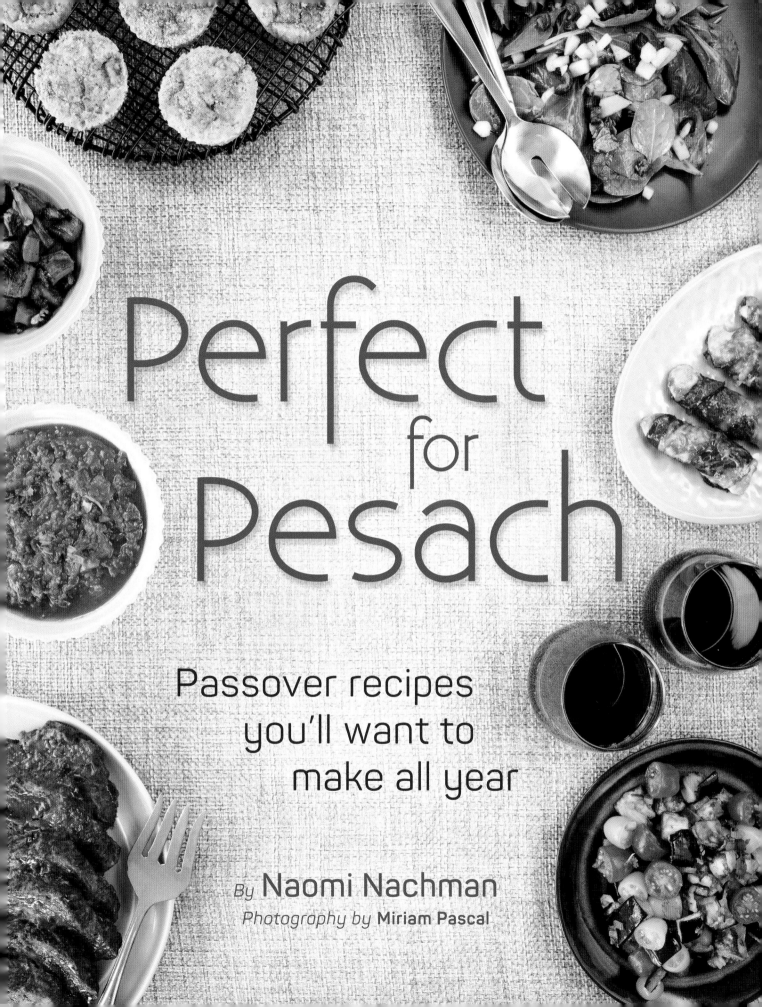

Perfect
for
Pesach

Passover recipes
you'll want to
make all year

By Naomi Nachman
Photography by **Miriam Pascal**

Published by **ARTSCROLL / SHAAR PRESS**
4401 Second Avenue / Brooklyn, NY 11232 / (718) 921-9000
www.artscroll.com

Distributed in Israel by **SIFRIATI / A. GITLER**
POB 2351 / Bnei Brak 51122 / Israel / 03-579-8187

Distributed in Europe by **LEHMANNS**
Unit E, Viking Business Park, Rolling Mill Road
Jarrow, Tyne and Wear, NE32 3DP / England

Distributed in Australia and New Zealand by **GOLDS WORLD OF JUDAICA**
3-13 William Street / Balaclava, Melbourne 3183, Victoria / Australia

Distributed in South Africa by **KOLLEL BOOKSHOP**
Northfield Centre / 17 Northfield Avenue / Glenhazel 2192
Johannesburg, South Africa

ISBN-10: 1-4226-1867-6 / ISBN-13: 978-1-4226-1867-7

Printed in Canada

Acknowledgments

> First and foremost, I would like to thank Hashem for all He has bestowed on me and my family. I feel so blessed by Him.

> I could not have written this book without the support and encouragement of my husband, Zvi Nachman, and my children, Simi and Raphy Sassieni, Eliana, Gabriella, and Leora. Thanks for being there every step of the way and for putting up with my crazy foodie adventures.

> Thank you to my wonderful parents, Miriam and Jack Stein of Sydney Australia, who raised me to be the foodie I am today, and to my grandmother, Rebecca Atlas, a"h, for showing me how exciting food can be. She would whiz around her tiny kitchen and whip up a feast in just a few hours.

> I am so grateful to Miriam Pascal, my amazing, super-talented photographer and friend, who helped me and held my hand throughout this process. What a fabulous ride this has been with you by my side.

> Thank you to Rabbi Meir Zlotowitz, Gedaliah Zlotowitz, Mendy Herzberg, Felice Eisner, Devorah Cohen, Judi Dick, Tova Ovits, and the entire talented team at ArtScroll for believing in me and making this book and my dream come to fruition.

> This book would not have been possible without my production team headed by Melinda Strauss, who is my foodie partner-in-crime. From catering, blogging and conferences, to foodie adventures, photography and advice, you have stood by me and have been a true friend in need.

> A special thanks to: Shana Aaron, Chanie Apfelbaum, Marilyn Atlas, Eitan Bernath, Miriam Blander, Reva Blander, Leah Jaroslawicz, Elizabeth Kurtz, Ella Kurtz, Chaya Suri Leitner, and Silvia Vargas, who each helped me shop, cook, recipe test, recipe develop, clean up, and keep me organized over the last several months.

> I also want to thank the following, who have always supported my brand: Gourmet Glatt, including Yoeli Steinberg, Moshe Ratner, Howie Klagsbrun, and Mendy Herz, who are always there for me. You make my food shopping and my culinary life so exciting. I'm so honored to be part of the Gourmet Glatt family.

> I am also grateful to all the companies that supported my brand and continue to work with me, including: Marzipan Bakery; Natural and Kosher Cheeses; Grow and Behold Meats; Abeles and Heymann; and Ram Caterers. Thank you for your continued support.

> A big thanks to *Mishpacha Magazine* and *The Jewish Home* for believing in me and making me part of your team.

> Thank you to Nachum Segal for giving me a voice and to Miriam L. Wallach for discovering me and getting me started as a radio host on *Table for Two with Naomi Nachman* (at www.nachumsegal.com). I am forever grateful to you both and the amazing team at the Nachum Segal Network.

> A special thank-you to Ariella Gelbtuch and Atara Habib for being unbelievable neighbors and for letting me raid your house for ingredients as well as for the endless babysitting, and to Rivka Boim, who has been by my side since we were 12 years old.

> Deena Fuchs and Naomi Ross: thank you for always proofreading my work and for your friendship over the years.

> Thank you, Beth Warren, MS, RDN, CDN, founder of Beth Warren Nutrition, for your help with the health facts about the oils.

> Robbie Schonfeld, a"h, of Ossie's Fish, who passed away while I was writing this book. Robbie gave me my start as a cooking teacher and recipe writer for Ossie's Fish when I first started my business. I am dedicating the fish chapter to his memory.

Table of Contents

Introduction
Why did I write a Pesach cookbook?

I grew up with Pesach being a main focus during the year. My parents ran a Pesach hotel program out of Sydney, Australia for 28 years — so as a family we were always very Pesach-centric.

Before my parents started their hotel program, my dad would entertain my brother and me while my mother and grandmother would make large batches of matzah balls, homemade gefilte fish, and so many cakes for Pesach. I was always amazed by how much food these two ladies could produce without any help.

One year, my mother was so exhausted from her Pesach preparations for our extended family that she passed out at our Seder. My father then decided that it was time for a new approach and the following year he started the first Pesach hotel program in Australia. His program continued for nearly three decades before he retired and sold it.

After I got married, I couldn't always go back to Sydney with my young family for Pesach, so I had to figure out how to make Pesach all on my own. I started on the Lower East Side with my husband in a small one-bedroom apartment and a cookbook that someone gave me at my bridal shower. There, I whipped up a massive Pesach feast for us — and that was the beginning of my Pesach career.

I saw that I had a knack and a passion for cooking. About a decade later, I started my own Pesach catering business, **The Aussie Gourmet**, with recipes that I developed. Some of the following recipes are brand-new, created just for this book, and others I developed over the past 23 years. Since those early days in my Manhattan apartment, I have watched the kosher-for-Pesach ingredient industry grow tenfold. There are now thousands of gebrochts and non-gebrochts ingredients to enhance your Pesach cooking. I like to use fresh, simple and delicious combinations of ingredients that are always available. My recipes are Perfect for Pesach and they are also perfect for the entire year.

My goal is to help you prepare delicious meals without making the process too complicated or exhausting. I hope that that you enjoy using this book as much as I did writing it!

Naomi Nachman

Making It Perfect

My intention is to present recipes that are easy to make with ingredients that are generally easily accessible from your local supermarket or online.

Although Perfect for Pesach focuses on recipes and dishes that can be made for Pesach, all the recipes can be used for year-round meals. In some cases, you may want to convert some of the ingredients from the book to year-round ingredients; where necessary, the Cook's Tips will provide guidance.

Every finished dish is a reflection of the ingredients from which it is made. I try my best to use quality ingredients and to refrain from using ingredients such as margarine and soup mixes. This is important to me, as I always do my best to stay away from these ingredients throughout the year. Where possible, for maximum flavor, I recommend the use of fresh lemons and limes for juice. A lemon will yield 3-4 tablespoons of juice, while a lime will yield 2-3 tablespoons. I also recommend the use of fresh garlic, which has a stronger flavor than jarred, powdered or frozen garlic.

Similarly, I advise using fresh herbs (instead of frozen or dried herbs) whenever a recipe calls for them. In all of the recipes in this book, I only use kosher (coarse) salt (rather than table salt), because it has a better flavor and elevates the flavor of the food. The recipes in this book require the use of large eggs (rather than extra-large eggs). For desserts, I strongly recommend using good-quality chocolate, with a high cocoa content. All these ingredients will help make your food taste far superior.

Likewise, it is important to use **fresh spices** for maximum flavor whenever possible. You will notice throughout this book that I frequently use spices such as cumin and curry, which may be (so far!) unfamiliar to you as Pesach ingredients, since these have only become generally available for Pesach in the last several years. I ask that you put aside any hesitations you have and expand your palate — try new flavors and you may come to love them. Since Pesach spices are only used during a short period during the year, you will likely have leftover spices after Pesach is over, to be used on the following Pesach seasons. I recommend storing these during the rest of the year in airtight containers which should be placed in a cool, dry area. Nonetheless, since stored spices may lose their vibrancy over a long period of time, I try to replace my store of spices every 2 to 3 years. Alternatively, use the Pesach spices during the year and replace them the following year with fresh jars.

When choosing an **oil** to use in a recipe, note that each type of oil has different properties that make it great in different applications. Below is an explanation of some of the oils I like to use on Pesach and all year long. Nutritionist Beth Warren, MS, RDN, CDN, shares with us some of the health benefits of the following oils.

Olive oil is known for its distinctive flavor, which makes it a good option for salad dressings, sautéing onions and garlic, and dishes such as shakshuka. Olive oil has a number of health benefits, which is another reason it's so popular. However, olive oil will burn at a lower temperature than other oils, which means it isn't a good option for frying, especially at high temperatures. My favorite type of olive oil is extra virgin, which has the strongest flavor. If you don't like such a strong flavor, use light olive oil, which has a milder flavor, but still provides the health benefits. When substituted for saturated fats, monounsaturated fats, such as those in olive oil, can help to improve blood cholesterol levels, reducing risk for heart disease. Specifically, extra-virgin olive oil is also high in antioxidants called polyphenols that have been linked to heart health.

Cottonseed oil is often sold for Pesach as "vegetable oil" and is widely used by many people. I don't like to use this oil, because it isn't as healthy as some of the other oil options. It does have a relatively high smoking point, so it works well for frying.

Avocado oil is a really nice and flavorful option for salad dressings. Avocado oil is rich in heart-healthy monounsaturated fats. It's also high in vitamin E, which acts as an antioxidant in your body. Avocado oil's high smoke point make it a top choice in high heat cooking.

Safflower oil is a neutral (less-flavored) oil, so I use it when I don't want the distinctive flavor of olive oil. Safflower oil is better for frying than olive oil, but it will burn more easily than canola oil (which you're likely accustomed to using all year), so be careful not to let it get too hot. In general, this is my go-to Pesach oil, as it's healthier than cottonseed oil and neutral enough to use for any recipes. The linolenic and linoleic acids in safflower oil have been shown to potentially lower cholesterol, help prevent hardening of the arteries, and reduce the risk of heart disease.

Walnut oil is extracted from walnuts, as the name implies, and accordingly has some nice health benefits. It has a mild, slightly nutty flavor, and works well in desserts. Although it may have a higher price tag than other oils, it is well worth it for the nutrient benefits. Walnut oil is rich in plant-based omega-3 fats, providing a cardio-protective benefit. Research indicates that walnut oil offers a rich source for antioxidants, but use with caution if a family member or guest has nut allergies.

Coconut oil is very different from the other oils listed. It's solid at room temperature, which makes it a good replacement for butter or margarine as an ingredient and to keep recipes nondairy or pareve. Coconut oil does contain saturated fat, so it's best to keep your total saturated fat intake at or below 10% of your daily calories.

At the start of every class that I teach, I like to remind my audience and/or students that the recipes are only guidelines for the dishes. Find your own inner-chef and use the flavors and spices in amounts you like. Get the family involved and be passionate about what you make. It will be contagious and everyone will love the effort you put into the food. Have fun in the kitchen and it will show in the results!

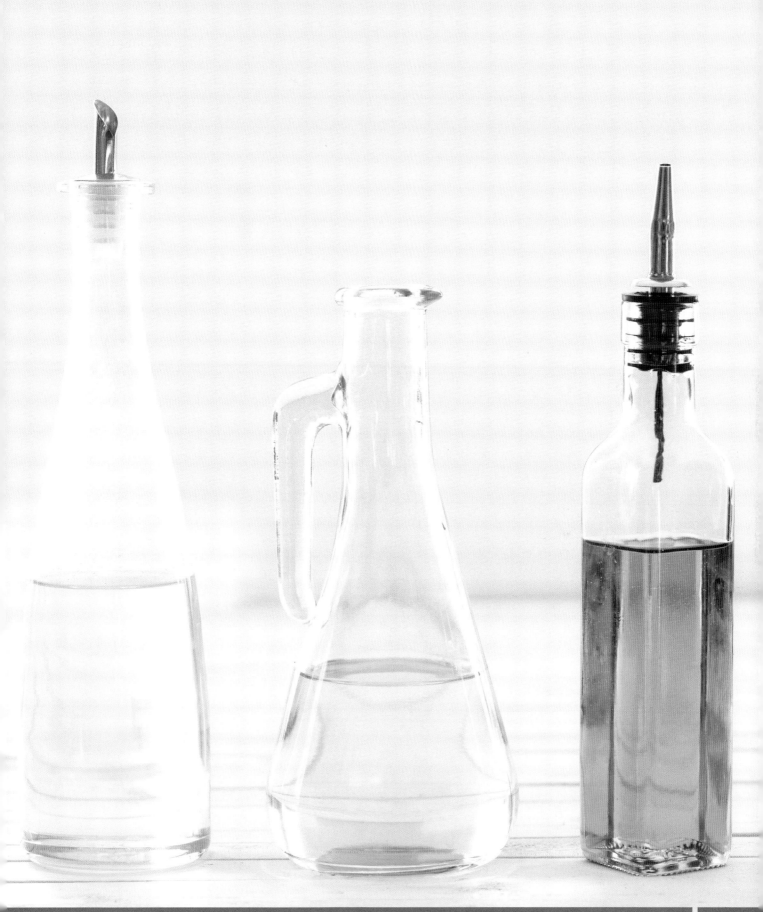

Basic Kitchen Equipment

This is my list of basic tools that are really handy to have on hand when setting up your Pesach collection. If you don't get everything the first year, don't worry — your collection will build over the years. As you receive houseware gifts over the course of the year or see great sales, think ahead to Pesach and put those items into your Pesach cabinet.

› **Food Processor**

I use this for so many things! Processing onions and garlic, shredding vegetables and potatoes for kugels, making sauces and salad dressings, and more.

› **Immersion Blender**

I use this to puree soups really quickly. Get a good-quality blender with a strong motor, because the cheap ones don't hold up well at all. If possible, have one for pareve and one for meat.

› **Large Frying Pan**

This is used for making shnitzel, breaded eggplant, stir fry, fried fish, and many other stovetop dishes. If possible, it's great to have one for pareve and one for meat.

› **Measuring Spoons and Measuring Cups**

For precise baking, it's important to measure carefully.

› **Metal Mixing Bowls**

I never have enough mixing bowls when there's a lot of cooking going on. It's good to have lots of them, in an assortment of sizes. I like metal because it cleans well (unlike plastic) and the bowls are more durable than glass.

› **9-Inch Nonstick Crepe Pan**

For best results when making crepes, use a nonstick crepe pan. It's important to use the crepe pan for crepes only, nothing else. To keep it functional, make sure to wash it with your fingers, not a sponge or steel wool.

› **Sharp Knives and Bamboo Cutting Boards**

Don't worry about getting expensive knives, but make sure your knives are sharp, which will make cutting and chopping much easier. Bamboo is my preferred material for cutting boards.

› **Sieve**

Useful for skimming scum from soup, as well as pushing avocado or boiled potato through to make a really creamy mash.

› **16-Quart Soup Pot**

This is great to make a huge batch of chicken soup to last all Pesach.

› **Stand Mixer or Hand Mixer**

A stand mixer is really useful for Pesach, for whipping egg whites, making cakes and cookies, and more. A hand mixer will work as well, but requires more effort on your part.

› **Swiss Y peelers**

I find the shape of these easiest to use, which is a good thing when there's so much peeling to do over Pesach. They also stay sharp longer than other types of peelers. I usually buy a few at a time.

› **Whisk**

Really important for making crepes, batters, salad dressings, and more.

› **Wooden Spoons**

They're great options because they are sturdy and don't scratch your pans while stirring.

Freezer Tips

There are three major rules to help ensure that your reheated food tastes fresh and delicious:

(1)

While defrosting in the oven, keep an eye on the food at all times as it can easily become dried out if left in too long.

(2)

Make sure freezer doors are always tightly closed (you'd be surprised how often something gets caught in the door, breaking the seal).

(3)

Everything should be covered with heavy duty foil or double-wrapped in regular foil; it's a good idea to then place it in a ziplock bag, labeled with item name and date.

My general rule is: **fish** can be frozen for up to one month; **chicken** for up to three months; and **meat** for up to six months.

Everyone's oven is different and people like to keep their ovens on at different temperatures during Yom Tov. Here are some general guidelines:

Meat

Take the meat out the day before serving to start the defrosting process and immediately place into the fridge. Up to an hour before the meal, place the meat into the oven at 250-275°F until the center is warmed through. Don't overcook the meat or it will dry out. Keep meat covered in the oven when reheating. Some cuts of meats (such as shoulder roast, London broil, duck, and lamb) are best served on the rarer side. If you prefer the meat well-done, leave it in the oven longer, until it is no longer pink in the center. Keep in mind that even once the oven is turned off, the carry-over heat will continue to cook and dry out any meat still in the oven.

Fried Food (Chicken, Fish, Egg Rolls)

Remove the food from the freezer 1 hour before frying and leave on counter to defrost at room temperature.

Chicken and Kugel

These should always go straight from freezer to oven, which should be set to a low to medium temperature (250-275°F). Don't let the kugel or chicken defrost first, as it will become soggy. Once in the oven, keep covered for the first half hour, until warmed through; then uncover to help it crisp up. I always baste the chicken with the sauce once or twice during the re-warming process after it has started to warm in the oven.

Soup

Take the container out of the freezer the night before if serving for lunch (or in the morning, if you are planning to serve the soup for dinner) and put it in the fridge. If you forget to defrost your soup ahead of time, take off the cover and run the container under hot water to release the frozen soup. Place into a pot on the stove over low heat until it thaws, then bring it to a boil. Stir soup as it comes to a boil. After it comes to a boil, taste it, as sometimes it may need to be re-seasoned. Each quart of soup usually serves 4 people. I also apply these rules to meatballs.

How to Prepare
Zucchini Noodles

pareve

INGREDIENTS

3 zucchini

METHOD

1 Use a julienne peeler or spiralizer to cut zucchini into long, thin, spaghetti-shaped strands.

2 Place the zucchini noodles in a single layer on paper towels. Let them air dry for at least 1 hour, up to 4 hours.

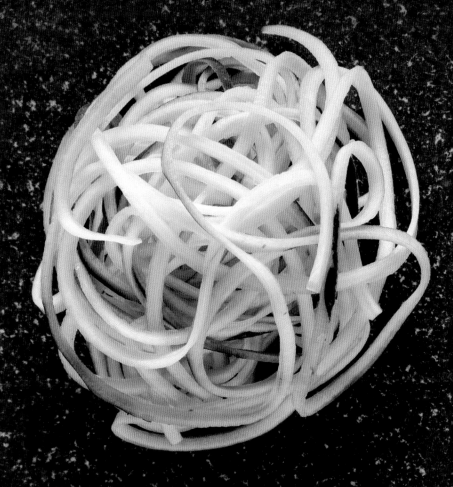

How to Prepare
Spaghetti Squash

pareve

INGREDIENTS

1 spaghetti squash

METHOD

1 Preheat oven to 375°F. Line a baking sheet with parchment paper; set aside.

2 Halve squash lengthwise; scoop out seeds.

3 Lay halves, flesh side down, on prepared baking sheet.

4 Bake **35** minutes or until you can easily pierce rind with a fork.

5 Remove squash from oven and set aside to cool.

6 Use a fork to scrape the squash flesh crosswise, pulling the strands from the rind.

How to Prepare
No-Flip Pesach Crepes

pareve – yields 12 crepes – freezer friendly

INGREDIENTS

12 eggs
6 Tablespoons potato starch
1 teaspoon salt
1 cup water

Cook's Tip

It's very important to use a 9-inch crepe pan for this recipe, and to treat it well. Use it for nothing besides crepes, and wash it with warm water and soap, using your fingers. Don't use a harsh brush that can ruin the surface.

Prepare Ahead

This recipe can easily be doubled. Store crepes in the freezer between layers of parchment paper.

METHOD

1 Combine all ingredients in a medium bowl. Beat well (preferably using a hand mixer).

2 Heat a 9-inch nonstick frying pan or crepe pan over medium heat. Coat pan with nonstick cooking spray.

3 Pour enough batter into the pan to **just** cover it, about ⅓-cup. Gently swirl the pan to coat the entire bottom with batter. Cook until the top is just set and the crepe is cooked through. Remove from pan to cool.

4 Repeat with remaining batter.

Appetizers

Cauliflower Crust Lachmagine

meat – yields 12 servings – freezer friendly

INGREDIENTS

Cauliflower Crust

2 (32-ounce) bags frozen cauliflower, defrosted

2 eggs

½ teaspoon salt

1 teaspoon onion powder

1 teaspoon dried oregano

Meat Topping

1 pound ground beef

1 cup prune butter or plum jam

1 small onion, diced

¼ cup tomato paste

½ cup ketchup

1 teaspoon salt

⅛ teaspoon cinnamon

1 cup pine nuts, optional

I've always enjoyed serving — and eating! — lachmagine, a Syrian meat pizza mezze, or appetizer. With cauliflower crust pizza so popular these days, I was inspired to try a cauliflower crust lachmagine for Pesach. I debuted it at the VIP Ram Pesach program (where I run cooking classes), and the Sephardic guests gave this recipe a thumbs-up for authentic flavor!

METHOD

1 **Prepare the crust:** Shred the cauliflower in a food processor until it resembles small crumbs.

2 Tightly wrap the cauliflower crumbs in a clean dish towel. (I divide the crumbs in half and use a separate dish towel for each half.) Squeeze the towel until the crumbs are dry. If the cauliflower is still cold from the freezer, let it sit out for 20 minutes and squeeze it again. The cauliflower should be very dry or the crust will become soggy.

3 Place the dry crumbs into a bowl; add eggs, salt, and spices. Mix really well until a "dough" forms.

4 Preheat oven to 400°F. Line a baking pan with parchment paper; set aside.

Cook's Tip

• For a dairy meal, make mini pizzas: Prepare the cauliflower crust through Step 5; add pizza sauce and cheese; bake in a preheated oven until cheese melts.

• See page 192 for instructions on how to prepare this with fresh cauliflower.

Prepare Ahead

Prepare recipe through Step 5, then freeze. Defrost, add the meat, and bake.

Year 'Round

When making this recipe during the year, see page 235 for non-Passover alternatives.

5 Form ¼-cup dough into a 2-3-inch round; place onto prepared pan. Repeat with remaining dough. Bake for 15 minutes, until they start to brown. Remove pan from oven.

6 **Meanwhile, prepare the meat topping:** Add all topping ingredients to a large bowl, mixing well to combine.

7 Reduce oven temperature to 350°F. Spread ¼-cup meat topping onto each baked round, pressing down so it sticks to the dough. Make sure to spread topping all the way to the edge, as the meat shrinks while it cooks. Sprinkle a few pine nuts on each, if using.

8 Bake until the meat is cooked through and browned, approximately 30 minutes.

Southwestern Chicken Egg Rolls

meat – yields 12 egg rolls – freezer friendly

INGREDIENTS

1 Tablespoon oil

1 medium onion, diced

4 chicken bottoms, bone-in, cooked and shredded (see Cook's Tips below)

¾ cup barbecue sauce

½ cup salsa

12 No-Flip Pesach Crepes (page 14)

• oil, for frying

A good chef or home cook never wants to waste anything, so I'm always looking for ways to use the chicken from my soup. This delicious Pesach appetizer is one of my favorite ways to make sure nothing goes to waste. The tangy salsa and sweet barbecue sauce are a surprisingly perfect combination.

METHOD

1. Prepare the filling: In a large frying pan, heat oil over medium heat. Add onion; sauté, stirring occasionally, until softened, approximately 5 minutes. Add chicken, barbecue sauce, and salsa; stir to combine until heated through.

2. Place approximately ¼ cup filling into the center of each crepe; fold bottom of crepe over filling. Fold in sides; roll up to the top edge to form egg rolls.

3. Heat oil to coat the bottom of a frying pan; fry the egg rolls for approximately 2 minutes per side, until crispy.

Cook's Tip

• Most people I know make chicken soup for Pesach — this is the best way to repurpose the chicken from it! If you normally don't include chicken quarters in your soup, add them to your regular recipe especially to make these egg rolls.

• Turn this into a Southwestern Chicken Soup! Add four cups chicken broth to the chicken mixture, bring it to a boil, and serve.

Year 'Round When making this recipe during the year, see page 235 for non-Passover alternatives.

Beef-Wrapped Chicken Fingers

meat – yields 1 dozen

INGREDIENTS

1-1½ pounds skinless, boneless chicken breasts, cut into 1-inch strips

2 (3-ounce) packages beef fry

½ cup duck sauce

2 cloves garlic, crushed

1 Tablespoon imitation soy sauce

1 Tablespoon sweet red wine

Smoked foods are all the rage nowadays, and smoky-tasting beef fry is increasing in popularity as well. These chicken fingers are infused with incredible flavors from the beef fry and the glaze, creating the perfect pairing.

METHOD

1 Preheat oven to 400°F. Line a baking sheet with parchment paper.

2 Wrap each chicken finger in a strip of beef fry; try to completely cover the chicken. Place wrapped chicken fingers onto prepared baking sheet, seam-side down.

3 In a small bowl, whisk together duck sauce, garlic, soy sauce, and wine.

4 Brush a generous amount of sauce over each chicken finger.

5 Bake for approximately 7 minutes. Flip fingers to second side; brush again with sauce, then bake for additional 7-8 minutes.

Cook's Tip
Double the sauce and reserve half to serve as a dipping sauce. Be sure not to contaminate the dipping sauce with the raw chicken.

Prepare Ahead
Wrap the raw chicken fingers and freeze. Defrost; add sauce just before baking.

Hush Puppy
Potato Knishes

meat – yields 24 knishes – freezer friendly

INGREDIENTS

6 large Idaho potatoes, peeled and cut into chunks

4 teaspoons kosher salt, divided

4 eggs, divided

3 Tablespoons potato starch

3 Tablespoons mayonnaise

½ teaspoon garlic powder

pinch white pepper

2-3 hot dogs, cut into half-inch pieces

When I was working on recipe development for Abeles and Heymann (a sponsor of my radio show on the Nachum Segal Network), I came up with this great way to put hot dogs into a fun and delicious appetizer. While hush puppies traditionally are made with dough, I kept mine "dough-less" so they would be gluten free — and therefore "Perfect for Pesach."

METHOD

1 Place potatoes, 1 teaspoon salt, and water to cover into a medium pot. Bring to a boil; cook until fork tender. Drain well.

2 Mash the potatoes well in a large bowl.

3 Add 3 eggs, potato starch, mayonnaise, garlic powder, remaining 3 teaspoons salt, and pepper, mixing well to combine. Set aside.

4 Preheat oven to 350°F. Line a baking sheet with parchment paper.

5 Scoop out ¼-cup mounds of potato mixture; place them on prepared baking sheet. Press a piece of hot dog into the center of each potato mound until it's completely covered.

6 Whisk the remaining egg to make an egg wash. Brush each potato mound with the egg wash.

7 Bake for approximately 40-50 minutes, until the potato mound starts to brown.

Cook's Tip

For pareve knishes, simply omit the hot dogs.

Shepherd's Pie Potato Skins

meat – yields 8-12 servings

INGREDIENTS

8 red potatoes, with peel, cleaned well

Meat Filling

1 Tablespoon oil

1 small onion, finely diced

2 cloves garlic, crushed

1 medium carrot, peeled and shredded

1 pound ground beef

3 Tablespoons ketchup

1 teaspoon kosher salt

Potato Topping

2 Tablespoons oil

1 teaspoon kosher salt

¼ teaspoon black pepper

1 egg

½ teaspoon paprika

Prepare Ahead

Meat filling can be made ahead and frozen.

Year 'Round

When making this recipe during the year, see page 235 for non-Passover alternatives.

My photographer, Miriam Pascal, and I had a great time playing around in the kitchen as we prepared food for the photo shoots. Together we came up with this incredible appetizer that will look really pretty on your holiday table.

METHOD

1   Preheat oven to 400°F. Line a baking sheet with parchment paper.

2   Place potatoes on prepared baking sheet. Bake for 50-60 minutes, until tender. Set aside until cool enough to handle.

3   **Meanwhile, prepare the meat filling:** Heat oil in a large frying pan over medium heat. Add onion; cook for approximately 5 minutes, until soft. Add garlic and carrot; sauté for an additional 2-3 minutes, until softened.

4   Add beef; cook, stirring to break up the meat, until meat is browned. Add ketchup and salt. Reduce heat to low; cook for approximately 10 minutes, until meat is cooked through. Set aside.

5   **Prepare the potato skins:** Cut each baked potato in half and scoop most of the potato flesh into a small bowl, leaving a small amount attached to the skin. (This will help the skin hold its shape.) Return potato skins to baking sheet.

6   **Prepare the potato topping:** Add oil, salt, pepper, and egg to reserved potatoes. Mash until smooth. Set aside.

7   **Assemble the potato skins:** Fill each potato skin with meat mixture, then spoon or pipe mashed potatoes over it. Sprinkle paprika over potatoes.

8   Bake for approximately 20 minutes, until tops are golden.

Vegetable Egg Rolls

pareve – yields 12 egg rolls – freezer friendly

INGREDIENTS

1 Tablespoon oil

1 medium onion, diced

1 (14-ounce) bag shredded cabbage with carrots (coleslaw mix)

3 cloves garlic, crushed

1 teaspoon kosher salt

½ teaspoon ground ginger

1 Tablespoon imitation soy sauce

1 Tablespoon honey

12 No-Flip Pesach Crepes (page 14)

• oil, for frying

I often serve fish as an appetizer, but I always like to offer a non-fish option as well. Everyone loves Chinese food, so I came up with these Chinese-inspired egg rolls.

METHOD

1 Heat oil in a large frying pan over medium heat. Add onion; cook for approximately 5 minutes, until translucent.

2 Add cabbage with carrots and garlic; cook for approximately 10 minutes, stirring occasionally.

3 Add salt, ginger, soy sauce, and honey. Taste; adjust seasonings. Set aside until cool enough to handle.

4 Place ¼-cup mixture onto the center of a crepe. Fold up, egg roll style (see page 18); repeat with remaining filling and crepes.

5 Heat oil to cover the bottom of a large frying pan over medium heat.

6 Fry egg rolls for a minute or two per side, until crispy and golden.

Year 'Round

When making this recipe during the year, see page 235 for non-Passover alternatives.

Prepare Ahead

Prepare egg rolls and freeze them between layers of parchment paper. Before frying, defrost and fry fresh.

Cook's Tip

To keep the oil from burning, add a piece of carrot to the pan while frying the egg rolls. The carrot will burn as it absorbs the blackened bits, keeping the oil clear.

Cauliflower Sushi

pareve – yields 4-5 rolls

INGREDIENTS

Cauliflower "Rice"

2 (32-ounce) bags frozen cauliflower, defrosted

1 teaspoon sugar

½ teaspoon kosher salt

1 teaspoon imitation soy sauce

1 teaspoon vinegar

Filling Options

- avocado
- carrot
- cucumber
- mango
- kani sticks, if available
- raw salmon, sushi-grade
- raw tuna, sushi-grade
- smoked salmon

Assembly

4-5 nori (seaweed) sheets

Who doesn't love sushi?! Even though Ashkenazic Jews don't eat rice on Pesach, that shouldn't stop anyone from enjoying sushi all Pesach long! Cauliflower rice is the perfect substitute, and it has the added benefit of making the sushi low-carb. Omit the nori and toss the other ingredients together to make this into a sushi salad.

METHOD

1 **Prepare the "rice":** Grate cauliflower in a food processor fitted with the "S" blade until it resembles small crumbs. Transfer the cauliflower crumbs to 2 clean dish towels.

2 Tightly wrap the cauliflower in the towels; squeeze dry. If it's still cold from being frozen, let it sit out for another 20 minutes and squeeze again. Make sure the cauliflower is very dry.

3 Place the cauliflower into a bowl; add sugar, salt, imitation soy sauce, and vinegar. Mix well; set aside.

4 **Prepare the filling:** Cut the fillings of your choice into long, thin strips. Place each filling component into a separate bowl.

Prepare Ahead

You can make the cauliflower rice 1 day in advance. Store in the fridge in an airtight container.

Cook's Tip

- Serve this sushi with imitation soy sauce or prepare Spicy Mayo: Mix ¼ cup mayo with sriracha to taste.

- You can use cooked quinoa instead of cauliflower rice in this recipe.

- See page 192 for instructions on how to prepare this with fresh cauliflower.

5 **Assemble the sushi rolls:** Place a nori sheet onto a bamboo mat. Spread the "rice" over the nori, forming into a thin layer and leaving a ½-inch border at the top edge.

6 Place the filling lengthwise along the center of the sheet. Don't overstuff with filling or the nori won't seal when you roll it.

7 Roll the nori, using the bamboo mat as a guide, pressing forward to shape into a cylinder. Press firmly to seal the roll. You may want to dampen the edge of the nori with water to help seal the roll.

8 Use a damp knife to cut sushi roll into 1-inch slices.

Seafood Cakes

pareve – yields 10 servings – freezer friendly

INGREDIENTS

1 (22-ounce) loaf gefilte fish, defrosted

2 Tablespoons curry powder, optional

1 teaspoon dried cilantro

1 Tablespoon dried dill

½ teaspoon cayenne pepper

1 Tablespoon prepared white horseradish

1 red pepper, finely diced

2 cups Pesach panko crumbs, divided

• oil, for frying

Ever since I was a little kid, I loved gefilte fish. I have fond memories of watching my grandmother prepare big bowls of gefilte fish by hand. This recipe is another way to enjoy this classic food as a modern appetizer, or a perfect seudah shelishit dish.

METHOD

1. In a large mixing bowl, combine fish, curry powder (if using), cilantro, dill, cayenne, horseradish, red pepper, and half the panko crumbs. Mix well.

2. Place remaining crumbs into a shallow bowl.

3. Form the mixture into patties approximately the size of your palm; then coat both sides in panko crumbs. Place onto a platter lined with parchment paper; to set the crumbs, refrigerate for 1 hour before frying.

4. Heat oil over medium-high heat in a large skillet. Fry the patties for 2-3 minutes per side, until cooked through. Drain fried patties on paper towels.

5. Serve with Remoulade Dipping Sauce, below.

Cook's Tip

• Curry is newly available for Pesach, and it's a great way to boost the flavor of your food.

• This recipe yields plenty of sauce. Set some aside to use as a dip for schnitzel as well.

Prepare Ahead

Make the seafood cakes up to one month in advance and freeze them in an airtight container.

Remoulade Dipping Sauce

INGREDIENTS

1¼ cups mayonnaise

2 teaspoons prepared white horseradish

1 teaspoon pickle juice or vinegar

1 teaspoon hot sauce, optional

¼ cup ketchup

1 large clove garlic, crushed

1 Tablespoon sweet paprika

METHOD

1. Whisk all ingredients together in a bowl until combined.

2. Serve with Seafood Cakes. Sauce remains fresh in the fridge for up to 7 days.

Guacamole Deviled Eggs

INGREDIENTS

6 eggs

1 avocado

1 Tablespoon lemon juice

½ teaspoon salt

¼ teaspoon onion powder

¼ teaspoon garlic powder

• fresh parsley sprigs, for garnish

When I was growing up, my mother would put eggs in her guacamole, so I flipped it around and put avocado into my eggs!

METHOD

1 Place eggs into a medium saucepan; cover eggs completely with cold water. Bring the water to a boil over high heat, covered. As soon as the water boils, turn off heat and let stand, covered, for 11 minutes (see Cook's Tip, below). Run cold water over the eggs for a couple of minutes, until cooled. Transfer the eggs to a bowl of ice water to cool completely.

2 Carefully peel the hard-boiled eggs; cut them in half lengthwise. Scoop the yolks into a mixing bowl. Place the egg whites onto a serving platter; set aside.

3 Cut the avocado in half; remove the pit. Scoop the avocado flesh into the mixing bowl with the egg yolks. Mash together the avocado and yolks. Sprinkle with the lemon juice, salt, onion powder, and garlic powder; stir to combine.

4 Scoop or pipe a generous spoonful of the avocado mixture into the hollow of each egg white. Garnish with a sprig of fresh parsley.

Cook's Tip

• The above method for cooking eggs yields perfect hard-boiled eggs without that green rim around the outside of the yolk, which is caused by the sulfur in the egg yolk separating if the eggs are boiled rapidly or too long. Use it here or any time you want hard-boiled eggs.

• To make the yolk mixture really smooth and velvety, push the yolks through a fine-mesh sieve, then add remaining ingredients.

Spinach-Stuffed Mushrooms

pareve – yields 8 servings

INGREDIENTS

8 Portobello mushrooms

1 Tablespoon olive oil

1 medium onion, diced

2 cloves garlic, crushed

16 ounces cremini or baby bella mushrooms, sliced

1 (24-ounce) bag frozen chopped spinach, defrosted and squeezed dry

½ teaspoon kosher salt

1 Tablespoon lemon juice

This is a light, low-fat appetizer, which is a great way to offset the heavy meals that are traditional on Pesach.

METHOD

1 Preheat oven to 400°F. Line a baking sheet with parchment paper.

2 Cut off Portobello mushroom stems; chop and set aside. Remove and discard mushroom gills.

3 Place Portobello mushroom caps on baking sheet; coat with nonstick cooking spray. Bake for 15 minutes. Remove from oven. Set aside. Do not turn off oven.

4 **Meanwhile, prepare the stuffing:** Heat olive oil over medium heat in a large frying pan. Add onion; sauté for 5-8 minutes, until translucent.

5 Add garlic, cremini mushrooms, and reserved chopped mushroom stems; sauté for 5-8 minutes.

6 Add spinach, salt, and lemon juice. Cook until the liquid from the spinach cooks off, approximately 10 minutes.

7 Divide stuffing among the Portobello mushroom caps; return to oven. Roast for 10 minutes.

Prepare Ahead

The filling can be made ahead and frozen. Then defrost before roasting and stuffing the fresh Portobello mushrooms.

Cook's Tip

• For a dairy meal, crumble feta cheese on top.

• Substitute shredded broccoli for the spinach, if desired.

Hawaiian Poke

pareve – yields 6-8 servings

INGREDIENTS

1½ pounds sushi grade salmon fillet, cubed

½ pound sushi grade tuna fillet, cubed

½ cup lemon juice

½ cup lime juice

1 jalapeño pepper, seeded and finely chopped

2 Tablespoons olive oil

½ teaspoon kosher salt

½ teaspoon ground black pepper

½ medium red onion, thinly sliced

2 avocados, peeled, pitted, and diced

1 mango, diced (optional)

¼ cup fresh cilantro, chopped (optional)

I was lucky enough to travel with my husband to Hawaii, and I noticed poke being sold everywhere. I researched the recipe and interviewed a number of Hawaiian chefs to learn more about this dish. I learned that poke means "cut piece" or "small piece," named for the small pieces of fish that make up the base of the dish. Pronounced po-kay, this dish seems exotic to us, but is actually a Hawaiian comfort food.

METHOD

1 Combine salmon, tuna, lemon juice, lime juice, jalapeño, olive oil, salt, pepper, and onion in a medium bowl. Marinate, covered, in refrigerator for 2 hours.

2 Just before serving, add avocado and mango, if using, to the fish mixture; sprinkle with cilantro. Serve immediately.

Cook's Tip

Because the fish is served raw, be sure to use very fresh fish that was purchased that day.

Prepare Ahead

Prepare the marinade a day ahead of time. Marinate the fish the day you're serving it.

Dips and Salads

Quinoa "Hummus"

pareve – yields 1½ cups

INGREDIENTS

1 cup cooked quinoa

½ cup pine nuts

2 cloves garlic, crushed

juice of **1** lemon (2-3 Tablespoons)

½ teaspoon salt

½ teaspoon cumin

1 Tablespoon olive oil

¼ cup water

1 Tablespoon olive oil, for garnish

1 Tablespoon parsley, finely chopped, for garnish

• paprika, for garnish

I'm a big hummus person — I put it on everything (it's almost like my ketchup!). I didn't want to write a cookbook without a hummus recipe, so I thought of using quinoa to make a kosher l'Pesach version. I was so excited by the idea that I invited some foodie friends to taste-test as I played around with numerous batches and versions to create the perfect Pesach "hummus." Here's the version that we all voted the best.

METHOD

1. Place quinoa and pine nuts into the bowl of a food processor fitted with the "S" blade. Process until just blended.

2. Add remaining ingredients; continue to blend. Scrape down the sides and blend again, for approximately 30 seconds. Do not over-blend or the mixture will become gummy.

3. Transfer to a serving bowl. Garnish with olive oil and chopped parsley; sprinkle with paprika.

Cook's Tip

1 cup uncooked quinoa prepared according to package directions will yield at least 2 cups cooked quinoa. You can use the rest to make Quinoa Tabuli (page 62), or any other quinoa recipe.

Prepare Ahead

Store in an airtight container in the fridge for up to a week.

Year 'Round

When making this recipe during the year, see page 235 for non-Passover alternatives.

Guacamole

pareve – yields 2 cups

This classic recipe is something I make nearly every Shabbos, and it's "Perfect for Pesach," too!

INGREDIENTS

4 avocados, peeled and pitted

2 Tablespoons fresh lime juice

1 Tablespoon fresh lemon juice

1 small red onion, finely diced

2 Tablespoons fresh cilantro or parsley, finely chopped (optional)

1 clove garlic, crushed

¼ teaspoon hot sauce

• salt, to taste

• pepper, to taste

METHOD

1 Scoop avocado flesh into a large bowl. Mash until smooth.

2 Add remaining ingredients; mix well until combined.

Cook's Tip

• I like to make this in a food processor so that it becomes creamy and mousse-like.

• Add some diced tomato to add texture and flavor, if desired.

Matbucha

pareve – yields 4 cups – freezer friendly

Low-fat and tomato based — this delicious Israeli recipe is packed with flavor.

INGREDIENTS

1 Tablespoon olive oil

1 large onion, diced

4 cloves garlic, crushed

1 jalapeño pepper, seeded and diced, optional

1 (28-ounce) can crushed tomatoes

1 (14-ounce) can diced tomatoes, with their liquid

1 bunch cilantro or parsley, finely diced

1 teaspoon salt

¼ teaspoon black pepper

1 teaspoon cumin

2 Tablespoons sugar

pinch cayenne pepper

METHOD

1 Heat oil in a large sauté pan over medium heat. Sauté onion for 5 minutes, or until soft and translucent.

2 Add garlic and jalapeño, if using; continue to cook, stirring occasionally, until soft (approximately 5 more minutes).

3 Add crushed tomatoes, diced tomatoes with their liquid, cilantro, salt, pepper, cumin, sugar, and cayenne pepper. Simmer, stirring occasionally, for 20 minutes until reduced and flavors are concentrated. Taste; adjust seasoning, if needed.

When making this recipe during the year, see page 235 for non-Passover alternatives.

JANUARY
1

Year 'Round

Vegetarian Chopped Liver

pareve – yields 2 cups – freezer friendly

I love chopped liver, and this recipe that I learned from an Israeli chef allows me to enjoy "chopped liver" while staying pareve.

INGREDIENTS

1 Tablespoon oil

1 small onion, diced

1 medium eggplant, cut into 1-inch chunks

2 Tablespoons olive oil

1 teaspoon kosher salt

2 hard-boiled eggs, peeled

¼-½ cup mayonnaise

½ teaspoon salt, or to taste

Cook's Tip

For instructions on making perfect hard-boiled eggs, see Step 1 on page 32.

METHOD

1. Heat oil in a frying pan over medium heat. Add onion; sauté until browned, 5-10 minutes. Set aside to cool.

2. Heat oven to 400°F. Line a baking sheet with parchment paper.

3. Toss eggplant, oil, and salt together on prepared baking sheet. Roast for 40 minutes. Set aside to cool.

4. Add onions, eggplant, eggs, and mayonnaise to the bowl of a food processor fitted with the "S" blade. Puree until completely smooth. Alternatively, you can place ingredients into a large bowl and puree them with an immersion blender. Adjust salt to taste.

Salsa Verde

pareve – yields 3 cups

I'm a big fan of Mexican food, and ever since my friend introduced me to salsa verde, I make this twist on it nearly every week. If you can't find tomatillos, you can make this dip with tomatoes instead. The flavor will be different but still delicious.

INGREDIENTS

10 tomatillos, husked, stemmed, or **8** plum tomatoes, divided

4 scallions

1 jalapeño pepper, ribs and seeds removed

2 cloves garlic

½ cup (packed) fresh cilantro leaves

½ cup fresh lime juice, or more, to taste

1 teaspoon salt, or to taste

¼ teaspoon black pepper

METHOD

1. Set broiler to high. Line a baking sheet with foil.

2. Place half the tomatillos, the scallions, and the jalapeño on the baking sheet. Broil for 3-4 minutes, until they begin to char around the edges. Remove

scallions and jalapeños from the oven (as they cook faster), then turn tomatillos and broil on second side until slightly charred, 3-4 minutes.

3 Preheat oven to 375°F. Grease a roasting pan; set aside.

4 Transfer charred tomatillos to prepared roasting pan. Add remaining tomatillos to pan. Roast until all tomatillos are soft, approximately 12 minutes. Set aside to cool.

5 Place tomatillos, scallions, jalapeño, garlic, cilantro, lime juice, salt, and pepper into a blender or food processor fitted with the "S" blade. Puree until smooth. Adjust salt, to taste.

Mum's Marinated Eggplant

pareve – yields 1 pint – freezer friendly

My mum, Miriam Stein of Sydney, Australia, is famous for this eggplant dip. Once you start eating it, you can't stop!

INGREDIENTS

- vegetable oil, for frying
- **1 large** eggplant, with peel, cut into ¼-inch rounds
- **1 cup** ketchup
- **¼ cup** sugar
- juice of **½** lemon (about 2 Tablespoons)
- **4 cloves** garlic, crushed
- **¼ cup** fresh parsley, finely chopped
- salt, to taste
- black pepper, to taste

Cook's Tip

Fresh garlic, fresh parsley, and fresh lemon juice are essential to the flavor here, so don't substitute!

METHOD

1 Heat half an inch of oil in a large frying pan over medium heat; add several eggplant rounds. Do not crowd pan. Fry for 3-4 minutes, until medium brown; flip to fry second side until medium brown. Repeat with remaining eggplant rounds.

2 Place fried eggplant in a colander with a plate under it to let the oil drain for 1 hour.

3 **Prepare the marinade:** Place ketchup, sugar, lemon juice, garlic, and parsley into a small bowl; stir to combine. Add salt and pepper to taste.

4 Gently add the eggplant into the marinade, being careful not to break up the slices. For best results, marinate overnight in the fridge.

Olive Dip

pareve – yields 2 cups – freezer friendly

My husband enjoys olives, so I developed this dip especially for him.

INGREDIENTS

- **3 cloves** garlic, crushed
- **2 (19-ounce) cans** green pitted sliced olives, drained
- **1 (19-ounce) can** Israeli pickles, drained
- **½ cup** pickled red peppers (optional)
- **1 teaspoon** cumin, optional
- **¼ teaspoon** cayenne pepper
- **2 Tablespoons** olive oil
- **2 Tablespoons** mayonnaise

METHOD

1 Add all ingredients to the bowl of a food processor fitted with the "S" blade.

2 Pulse until very small pieces form, but don't overprocess until it's a paste. You want some texture to remain.

Lighten Up

Instead of frying the eggplant slices, cut eggplant into rounds or 1-inch cubes, sprinkle with salt and olive oil, and roast at 400°F about 40 minutes, until golden brown. Then continue with Step 3.

Charoset Salad

pareve – yields 8 servings

INGREDIENTS

Candied Almonds

1 cup blanched, sliced almonds

½ cup sugar

½ teaspoon cinnamon

Dressing

½ cup cream Malaga or sweet red wine

½ cup balsamic vinegar

¾ cup oil

2 Tablespoons sugar

1 teaspoon salt

¼ teaspoon cinnamon

pinch cayenne pepper

Salad

5-6 ounces baby spinach or choice of lettuce

3 Granny Smith apples, with peel, diced

8 dried dates, pitted and diced

My husband's job every Pesach is to make the charoset. He would eat it every day if he could. I wanted to include a version of charoset, but I decided to take it a step further, so I created this charoset-inspired salad with him in mind. It has all of the flavors you expect to find: cinnamon, wine, nuts, apples, and more.

METHOD

1 **Prepare candied almonds:** Line a baking sheet with parchment paper; set aside.

2 Heat a frying pan over medium heat. Add almonds, sugar, and cinnamon; cook for approximately five minutes, stirring frequently, until the sugar is dissolved — do not overcook or sugar will burn.

3 Spread the nuts in a single layer on prepared baking pan; set aside to cool.

4 **Prepare the dressing:** Combine all dressing ingredients in a container; cover tightly and shake to combine.

5 **Assemble the salad:** Add spinach, apples, dates, and candied almonds to a large bowl. Just before serving, drizzle with desired amount of dressing (you will have extra); toss to combine.

Prepare Ahead

Nuts can be stored in an airtight container at room temperature for about a week. Dressing can be prepared ahead and stored in the fridge for about a week.

Cook's Tip

• Be careful when working with the candied almonds, as hot sugar can cause a painful burn.

• This recipe makes a large quantity of dressing. Keep any extra in the fridge and use it to dress salads all week.

Kale and Roasted Butternut Squash Salad

pareve or meat – yields 8 servings

INGREDIENTS

Butternut Squash

1 small butternut squash, peeled, cut in 1-inch cubes

1 teaspoon salt

¼ teaspoon garlic powder

¼ teaspoon paprika

1 Tablespoon olive oil

Dressing

1 clove garlic, crushed

¼ teaspoon paprika

¼ cup balsamic vinegar

¼ cup sugar

½ teaspoon salt

¼ cup ketchup

¾ cup olive oil

Salad

1 bunch kale leaves, tough center stems removed, washed well, dried, and torn into bite-size pieces

½ cup dried cranberries

• candied beef or duck fry, optional (see Cook's Tip, below)

When kale first started to emerge as a superfood, I created this salad to showcase it. It's always a hit with my family, friends, and catering clients.

METHOD

1 **Prepare the butternut squash:** Preheat oven to 425°F. Line a baking sheet with parchment paper.

2 Place butternut squash cubes on prepared baking sheet. Sprinkle with salt, garlic, paprika, and oil. Toss to coat.

3 Roast for 45 minutes, until soft and the edges are turning brown. Set aside to cool.

4 **Prepare the dressing:** Whisk dressing ingredients together in a small bowl. Set aside.

5 **Assemble the salad:** Place kale into a large bowl. Add butternut squash, dried cranberries, and candied beef fry, if using. Add dressing; toss to combine.

Cook's Tip

To make candied fry, line a baking sheet with foil. Add 6 fry strips to prepared pan. Sprinkle with ¼ cup brown sugar. Bake at 350°F for 20 minutes, until crisp. Cut into small pieces; add to salad.

Arugula Pomegranate Salad

pareve – yields 6-8 servings

This salad is always a hit, not only because of its delicious, sweet, and tangy flavors, but because of its beautiful colors as well.

INGREDIENTS

Vinaigrette

¼ cup balsamic vinegar

1 clove garlic, crushed

¼ cup honey

½ cup olive oil

1 teaspoon salt

¼ teaspoon black pepper

Salad

6 cups arugula

1 avocado, peeled and cubed

1 mango, peeled and cubed

½ cup pomegranate seeds or dried cranberries

½ red onion, thinly sliced

1 jicama, peeled and cubed, optional

METHOD

1 **Prepare the vinaigrette:** Whisk together vinegar, garlic, and honey. While continuing to whisk, slowly drizzle in olive oil to emulsify the vinaigrette. Season with salt and pepper; adjust seasonings to taste.

2 Just before serving, toss arugula, avocado, mango, pomegranate seeds, red onion, and jicama, if using, with the dressing in a large bowl.

Cook's Tip

• If you can't find arugula, use baby spinach or romaine lettuce instead.

• I double my dressing so I always have fresh homemade dressing on hand.

• The vinaigrette will remain fresh for up to 1 week in the refrigerator in an airtight container.

Salad Niçoise

pareve – yields 6-8 servings

INGREDIENTS

Shallot Dressing

3 Tablespoons vinegar

1 small shallot

1 clove garlic

1 Tablespoon chopped fresh tarragon or **1 teaspoon** dried tarragon

¾ cup olive oil

• salt, to taste

• pepper, to taste

Salad

1 head Boston, soft butter, or romaine lettuce, torn into bite-size pieces

2 (6-ounce) cans tuna packed in oil, drained and broken into chunks

½ cup Niçoise olives, or your favorite olives

8 mini potatoes, with peel, boiled until fork tender, quartered

2 hard-boiled eggs, peeled and quartered

4 plum tomatoes, quartered

2 radishes or **1** watermelon radish (pictured), thinly sliced

The first time I had Salad Niçoise was when I was in Israel for seminary, and I've enjoyed it ever since. This is a great seudah shelishit salad because it's a full meal in a bowl. You can serve this on one big platter, or individually plated as an appetizer.

METHOD

1. **Prepare the dressing:** Place vinegar, shallot, garlic, and tarragon into the bowl of a food processor fitted with the "S" blade. Process until smooth.

2. With the machine still running, slowly add oil in a slow, steady stream to incorporate it into the dressing. Add salt and pepper to taste.

3. **Prepare the salad:** Line a platter with lettuce; top with tuna, olives, and potatoes. Arrange egg and tomato wedges around platter. Drizzle with shallot dressing; top with sliced radishes.

Cook's Tip
To really elevate the salad, use fresh seared tuna (as pictured) instead of canned. Season a ½-inch-thick tuna steak on all sides with salt and pepper. Sear in a skillet in a tablespoon of hot oil for two minutes per side; it will still be pink in the center. Slice and arrange on platter.

Year 'Round
When making this recipe during the year, see page 235 for non-Passover alternatives.

Skirt Steak Salad
with Caesar Dressing

meat – yields 8 servings

INGREDIENTS

During the summer, I make this salad every Shabbat for lunch, and it's always finished to the last bite. It will be a big hit at a Pesach lunch as well.

Marinated Skirt Steak

2 pounds (approximately) skirt steak, soaked (see Cook's Tip, below)

¼ cup olive oil

2 cloves garlic, crushed

Dressing

1 cup mayonnaise

2 cloves garlic, crushed

1 teaspoon fish-free imitation Worcestershire sauce

¼ cup fresh lemon juice

¼ teaspoon kosher salt

¼ teaspoon black pepper

Salad

6 cups romaine lettuce, torn into bite size pieces

1 pint cherry tomatoes, halved

½ cup terra sticks, optional

METHOD

1 **Prepare the meat:** Combine meat, oil, and garlic in a ziplock bag; marinate in the fridge for 2-4 hours.

2 Heat a grill pan over a medium-high heat. Remove meat from marinade. Discard remaining marinade. Grill steak for 4-5 minute per side, for medium rare. Set aside to cool completely.

3 **Prepare the dressing:** Whisk dressing ingredients together in a small bowl until combined.

4 **Assemble the salad:** Place lettuce and tomatoes into a large bowl. Cut steak into thin slices; add to bowl. Top with terra sticks, if using.

5 Add desired amount of dressing just before serving; toss to combine. Extra dressing will remain fresh in the fridge for up to one week.

Cook's Tip

Skirt steak is a very salty cut. Before marinating, soak the meat to cut the salt: Soak it in a bowl of water in the fridge for a few hours. Change the water every hour or so.

Lighten Up

Use grilled chicken or strips of deli turkey in place of the steak.

Year 'Round

When making this recipe during the year, see page 235 for non-Passover alternatives.

Goat Cheese Salad
with Raspberry Vinaigrette

dairy – yields 8 servings

INGREDIENTS

1 (10-ounce) log goat cheese, grated or crumbled

2 heads romaine lettuce, shredded, or greens of your choice.

1 small red onion, sliced into half-moons, optional

1 cup terra sticks

• choice of raspberry dressings, below

I rarely serve a dairy meal without including this salad! The combination of raspberry dressing and goat cheese is an amazing marriage of flavors.

METHOD

1 Place cheese, lettuce, onion, and terra sticks into a large bowl.

2 Just before serving, drizzle with dressing of your choice; toss to coat.

Cook's Tip

You may want to double the dressing and keep it in the fridge to dress salads of your choice all week long!

Quick & Easy Raspberry Dressing

INGREDIENTS

1 (16-ounce) bottle Italian dressing

1 (12-ounce) jar seedless raspberry jam

METHOD

› Use a food processor or immersion blender to combine dressing and jam until fully pureed.

Homemade Raspberry Dressing

INGREDIENTS

2 small shallots, peeled

6 Tablespoons raspberry preserves

¼ cup balsamic vinegar

⅔ cup olive oil

• salt, to taste

• ground black pepper, to taste

METHOD

1 Place shallots into a food processor fitted with the "S" blade; mince finely. Add preserves and vinegar.

2 While machine is running, add the oil slowly, in a steady stream.

3 Add salt and pepper to taste.

Israeli Salad
with Shawarma Chicken Cubes

meat ─ yields 6 servings

I'm always looking to put a modern twist on a traditional recipe. The chicken cubes really transform this salad into a hearty meal — perfect to take with you when you go on a Chol HaMoed trip (or a matzah picnic, as we call it in Australia).

INGREDIENTS

Shawarma Chicken Cubes

- **¼ cup** olive oil
- **5 cloves** garlic, sliced
- **1 teaspoon** cumin
- **½ teaspoon** cinnamon
- **1 teaspoon** kosher salt
- **1 teaspoon** paprika
- **1 pound** skinless boneless chicken cutlets

Salad

- **3-4** plum tomatoes, diced
- **1-2** seedless cucumbers, skin on, diced
- **½** red onion, peeled and finely chopped
- **½** yellow pepper, diced
- **¼ cup** assorted fresh herbs, such as mint, parsley, and cilantro, chopped

Dressing

- **½ cup** lemon juice (from about 2 lemons)
- **¼ cup** olive oil
- **1 teaspoon** kosher salt
- **¼ teaspoon** black pepper

METHOD

1. **Prepare the chicken cubes:** Place all cube ingredients into a ziplock bag; marinate in the fridge for 1-2 hours, up to overnight.

2. Preheat oven to 400°F. Line a baking sheet with parchment paper.

3. Remove cutlets from marinade; place cutlets on prepared baking sheet. Discard remaining marinade. Bake, uncovered, for 20 minutes, until cooked through. Set chicken aside to cool. Cut cooled chicken into bite-size cubes.

4. **Prepare the salad:** Place all vegetables into a large bowl. Add chicken cubes, herbs, lemon juice, olive oil, salt, and pepper. Toss to combine.

Prepare Ahead

Chicken can be marinated and frozen raw, then cooked 1 day ahead of time.

Cook's Tip

Omit the chicken to keep this salad pareve.

Year 'Round

When making this recipe during the year, see page 235 for non-Passover alternatives.

Mediterranean Eggplant Salad

pareve – yields 6 servings

INGREDIENTS

1 large eggplant, with peel, cut into 1-inch chunks

2 teaspoons kosher salt, divided

¼ cup olive oil

1 cup cherry tomatoes, halved

juice of **1** lemon

2 cloves garlic, crushed

½ teaspoon cumin, optional

2 Tablespoons olive oil

2 Tablespoons fresh cilantro or parsley, finely chopped

This salad is one that I make so often, it's gotten to the point that my guests know to expect this whenever they come for a meal.

METHOD

1 Preheat oven to 400°F. Line a baking sheet with parchment paper.

2 Toss eggplant with 1 teaspoon salt and oil on prepared baking pan. Roast for 40 minutes. Set aside to cool.

3 Combine cooled eggplant, tomatoes, lemon juice, garlic, cumin, and remaining teaspoon salt (or to taste) in a bowl. Drizzle with olive oil; add herbs and toss to combine.

Cook's Tip
Double the roasted eggplant mixture and add some to salads or bake with sauce and cheese to make an eggplant bake.

Prepare Ahead
Eggplant can be roasted up to two days in advance. Store, covered, in the fridge.

Quinoa Tabouli

pareve – yields 8-10 servings

INGREDIENTS

1 cup raw quinoa

5 plum tomatoes, chopped

1 small red onion, finely chopped

½ cup fresh parsley leaves, finely chopped

½ cup fresh lemon juice, or more, to taste

3 Tablespoons extra virgin olive oil

1 Tablespoon kosher salt, or to taste

¼ teaspoon white pepper (optional)

When I was growing up, my mother usually made tabouli for Shabbat. She made it the traditional way, with bulgur wheat. My cousin, Shelley Serber, introduced me to this updated version, using quinoa. Now I make it every week too, including on Pesach.

METHOD

1 Cook quinoa according to package directions.

2 In a large bowl, stir together cooked quinoa, tomatoes, red onion, and parsley.

3 Add lemon juice and olive oil; stir to combine. Season with salt and pepper, to taste.

Year 'Round

When making this recipe during the year, see page 235 for non-Passover alternatives.

Beet Salad
with Candied Nuts

— pareve – yields 8 servings —

Beets and tomatoes are a pairing that I enjoy often, and the sugared nuts really complete the dish by bringing out their sweetness.

INGREDIENTS

6 medium beets

1 Tablespoon olive oil

1 teaspoon kosher salt

¼ teaspoon black pepper

1 cup cherry tomatoes, halved

½ cup fresh parsley leaves, chopped

3 scallions, thinly sliced

• candied nuts (store-bought or homemade; see Cook's Tip below)

Dressing

½ cup balsamic vinegar

½ cup olive oil

¼ cup mayonnaise

• kosher salt

• freshly ground black pepper

METHOD

1 **Prepare the beets:** Preheat the oven to 400°F degrees. Line a baking sheet with parchment paper; set aside.

2 Remove the tops and the root ends of the beets. Peel beets; cut beets into 1-inch chunks.

3 Place the cut beets on prepared baking sheet; toss with olive oil, salt, and pepper. Roast for 35-40 minutes, turning once or twice with a spatula, until beets are tender. Set aside to cool.

4 **Meanwhile, prepare the dressing:** Place dressing ingredients into a bowl; whisk until the oil is incorporated. Add salt and black pepper to taste.

5 After beets have cooled, place them into a large bowl. Add tomatoes, parsley, scallions, nuts, and dressing. Toss to combine.

Prepare Ahead

Beets can be roasted ahead of time and stored in the fridge until you're ready to make the salad.

Year 'Round

When making this recipe during the year, see page 235 for non-Passover alternatives.

Cook's Tip

• Add cubes of roasted beets to your favorite salads for extra flavor and texture.

• If you make the candied almonds on page 46 for this recipe, omit the cinnamon.

Tropical Slaw

pareve – yields 6 servings

The flavors of this tropical-inspired salad evoke the taste of summer!

INGREDIENTS

1 mango, cubed

2 avocados, cubed

1 red onion, diced

½ cup pomegranate seeds

1 small head or **1 (10-ounce)** bag purple cabbage, shredded

Dressing

3 Tablespoons honey

½ cup olive oil

6 Tablespoons orange juice

1 teaspoon kosher salt, or to taste

METHOD

1 In a small bowl, whisk together all dressing ingredients until smooth. Pour dressing over cabbage; let it sit for 30 minutes.

2 Add remaining ingredients just before serving.

Cook's Tip If you don't have pomegranate seeds, you can use dried cranberries instead.

Chimichurri Coleslaw

pareve – yields 6 servings

INGREDIENTS

Chimichurri Dressing

¾ cup parsley leaves

2 cloves garlic

½ jalapeño pepper, seeds and ribs discarded

1 small shallot

juice of **2** limes (about ¼ cup)

½ cup olive oil

2 teaspoons kosher salt

1 (14-ounce) bag coleslaw mix

My friends, Miriam Pascal and Melinda Strauss, were at my house working on our photo shoot, and I mentioned that I needed to come up with an amazing slaw that's unique and perfect for Pesach. Working together, we developed this fantastic and flavor-packed version, making a chimichurri sauce as the dressing. This slaw is proof that three heads are better than one!

METHOD

1　**Prepare the dressing:** In the bowl of a food processor fitted with the "S" blade, puree all dressing ingredients until smooth.

2　Place coleslaw mix into a large bowl; toss with chimichurri dressing.

3　Let slaw sit for 15-20 minutes to marinate before serving.

Cook's Tip

• If you like your salad hot, use the ribs and seeds of the jalapeño, adding them to the food processor with the dressing ingredients.

• You can also use the dressing as a marinade for grilled chicken or served alongside a steak.

Erev Pesach Potato Salad

meat – yields 8 servings

My parents ran a Pesach program out of Sydney, Australia, for 28 years. Aside from my great memories of the program, I also fondly recall enjoying this potato salad at their yearly Erev Pesach buffet. With limited food options on Erev Pesach, I like to serve this salad — it's a delicious, filling meal. Serve this at your next barbecue.

INGREDIENTS

30 baby red potatoes or **6 large** red potatoes, with skin

1½ teaspoons salt, divided

3 Tablespoons fresh dill, chopped

1 cup assorted deli meats, shredded

4 sour pickles or Israeli pickles, sliced or cubed

¼ cup mayonnaise

2-3 scallions, sliced

METHOD

1 Place potatoes into a large pot with 1 teaspoon salt. Cover with water; bring to a boil. Cook until tender.

2 Cut the baby potatoes in half; if using large potatoes, cut them into quarters.

3 Add potatoes and remaining ingredients to a large bowl. Stir to combine.

Soups

Zucchini Mushroom Soup

pareve – yields 10-12 servings – freezer friendly

INGREDIENTS

1 large onion, diced

2 Tablespoons olive oil

5-6 cups cremini or baby bella mushrooms, sliced

4-6 medium zucchini, washed, with peel, cut into chunks

2 medium potatoes, peeled and cut in chunks

• water or vegetable stock

1 Tablespoon kosher salt, or to taste

¼ teaspoon white pepper, or to taste

This soup gets its richness from the mushrooms and its creaminess from the zucchini. Even though it is a rich soup, it's relatively low in calories.

METHOD

1 In a large (10-quart) soup pot, heat the oil over a medium heat. Add onions; sauté for a few minutes, until they begin to soften.

2 Add mushrooms; sauté for a few more minutes. Add zucchini and potatoes.

3 Add enough water to fill pot to just under vegetables. Don't add too much liquid, or soup will be too watery. Bring soup to a boil; reduce heat. Simmer until vegetables are soft, approximately 45 minutes.

4 Use an immersion blender to process soup for a full 3 minutes, until smooth. Season with salt and pepper, to taste.

Cook's Tip

• To make the fried mushroom garnish, fry slices of mushrooms in olive oil until crispy. Place onto soup just before serving.

• If you can't find cremini or baby bella mushrooms, use white mushrooms or an assortment of your choice.

Roasted Tomato Soup

pareve – yields 10 servings – freezer friendly

INGREDIENTS

8 plum tomatoes

2 Tablespoons olive oil, divided

½ teaspoon kosher salt

1 large onion, diced

2 large cloves garlic, crushed

1 (28-ounce) can crushed tomatoes

8 cups vegetable stock

½ teaspoon dried thyme

• kosher salt, to taste

• pepper, to taste

Growing up, I always loved tomato soup; my mum used to serve it on Sunday night at dinner. Now that I've grown up, I make my own version and I discovered that roasting the tomatoes deepens the flavors.

METHOD

1 Preheat oven to 400°F. Line a baking sheet with parchment paper; set aside.

2 Slice each tomato in half lengthwise; place, skin-side down, on prepared baking sheet. Drizzle with 1 tablespoon olive oil and salt.

3 Roast for 30 minutes or until tomatoes are caramelized; set aside.

4 Heat remaining tablespoon oil in a 4-quart soup pot over medium heat. Add onion and garlic; sauté for a few minutes, until translucent. Add roasted tomatoes; cook, stirring occasionally, for a few minutes.

5 Add crushed tomatoes, stock, and thyme; bring to a boil. Reduce heat to low; simmer for 30 minutes.

6 Use an immersion blender to process soup for a full 3 minutes, until smooth; add salt and pepper to taste.

Cook's Tip

For a dairy meal, add a handful of shredded cheese to each bowl; stir to melt cheese.

Kitchen Sink Vegetable Soup

pareve – yields 16 servings – freezer friendly

INGREDIENTS

Broth

1 large parsnip, peeled

1 turnip, peeled

4-5 stalks celery

2 medium zucchini, with peel

3 large onions

3 medium carrots

1 large tomato

8 cups water

½ cup fresh parsley leaves

½ Tablespoon kosher salt

Diced Vegetables

4 stalks celery, peeled

3 medium carrots, peeled

2 medium zucchini, with peel

2 onions

1 small parsnip, peeled

1 Tablespoon kosher salt

I made this soup for the first time because I had a whole bunch of vegetables that were about to go bad, so I decided to put them all into a soup. A chef I once worked with taught me the this trick for making a homemade soup base: blending the simmered vegetables and then using that stock to make an amazingly rich soup with the diced veggies.

METHOD

1 **Prepare the broth:** Cut parsnip, turnip, celery, zucchini, onions, carrots, and tomato into large chunks. Place into a large (10-quart) pot; add water, parsley, and salt.

2 Bring to a boil; reduce heat and simmer until vegetables are soft, approximately 1 hour.

3 Use an immersion blender to process soup for a full 3 minutes, until smooth. Reheat to a boil.

4 **Complete the soup:** Cut the remaining vegetables into small dice. Add to pureed soup; lower heat. Simmer for approximately 2 hours, until the vegetables are soft enough to your taste. Add salt; adjust to taste.

Cook's Tip

This is a perfect soup to use up any vegetables that you have laying around in your kitchen — hence the name! Some other vegetables you can throw in when making the broth are yellow squash, butternut squash, sweet potatoes, or beets. If you have mushrooms, dice them and add to the soup in Step 4.

Roasted Cauliflower and Garlic Soup

pareve – yields 4-6 servings – freezer friendly

This is a low-carb version of Potato Leek Soup. This is one of the most requested soups of my Pesach catering business

INGREDIENTS

Roasted Garlic

- **1 small head** garlic
- **1 teaspoon** olive oil
- **½ teaspoon** kosher salt
- **pinch** black pepper

Roasted Cauliflower

- **1 (32-ounce) bag** frozen cauliflower
- **2 Tablespoons** olive oil
- **1 teaspoon** kosher salt
- **pinch** black pepper

Soup

- **1 Tablespoon** olive oil
- **1 medium** onion, diced
- **2 medium** Yukon Gold potatoes, peeled and cut into chunks
- **3 medium** zucchini, with peel, cut into chunks
- **1 teaspoon** salt
- **¼ teaspoon** black pepper

Cook's Tip

Double the roasted garlic; squeeze some into mashed potatoes for incredible flavor. You can also spread the roasted garlic on matzah.

METHOD

1 **Prepare the roasted garlic and cauliflower:** Preheat oven to 375°F. Line a baking sheet with parchment paper.

2 Cut off the top of the head of garlic; place garlic head on a piece of foil. Sprinkle with oil, salt, and pepper. Wrap foil around garlic to seal. Place on prepared baking sheet.

3 Add cauliflower, oil, salt, and pepper to baking sheet. Toss to combine. Roast for 45 minutes, until cauliflower starts to brown. Set aside.

4 **Prepare the soup:** Heat oil in a medium pot over medium heat. Add onion; cook, stirring occasionally, for approximately 10 minutes, until soft.

5 Add roasted cauliflower, potatoes, zucchini, salt, and pepper. Unwrap the garlic; squeeze the roasted cloves into the pot. Add water just to cover the vegetables.

6 Bring to a boil; then reduce heat to low. Simmer for 45-60 minutes, until the vegetables are soft.

7 Use an immersion blender to process soup for a full 3 minutes, until smooth. Add water (approximately ½ cup) if necessary, until the soup has the consistency you prefer.

Matzah Balls

pareve – yields 18 small matzah balls – freezer friendly – gebrochts -

Most people just serve matzo balls with their chicken soup, but I love to serve them with all kinds of soup!

INGREDIENTS

1 cup matzah meal

4 eggs, lightly beaten

¼ cup oil

¼ cup water

2 teaspoons kosher salt

Cook's Tip

• Dampen your hands with water when rolling the balls so they don't stick to your hands.

• I like to replace the oil with duck fat (now available in a jar!) to make them more indulgent. My grandmother added a fried onion for extra flavor.

METHOD

1 Add all ingredients to a medium bowl; mix with a fork until just combined. Do not overmix or the matzah balls will be too hard. Place into refrigerator for approximately 30 minutes, until mixture is firm enough to form balls.

2 Bring a large pot of salted water to a boil.

3 Roll small amounts of the mixture between your palms to form balls (approximately the size of golf balls), and lower the balls into the water. Reduce heat to low (a rolling boil will cause the balls to break apart). Simmer for approximately 20 minutes, until cooked through. Remove with a slotted spoon.

Pesach Egg Noodles

pareve – yields 12 servings – freezer friendly

Making "eyere lukshen" (egg noodles) from Pesach crepes has been a tradition in my family for generations. Preparing something so traditional makes me feel connected to my past.

INGREDIENTS

1 batch No-Flip Pesach Crepes, prepared according to directions on page 14

METHOD

1 Roll 2-3 cooked crepes at a time into a tight roll; cut into slices, approximately ¼-inch wide.

2 Unroll resulting strips; serve in soup.

Flanken Butternut Squash Soup

meat – yields 12 servings – freezer friendly

INGREDIENTS

4 strips (2-2½ pounds) flanken

2 large onions, quartered

2 medium butternut squash, peeled, seeded, and cut into large chunks

4 large loose carrots, peeled and cut into large chunks

3 medium Yukon Gold potatoes, peeled and cut into large chunks

1 sweet potato, peeled and cut into large chunks

- salt, to taste
- pepper, to taste

I once had an amazing butternut squash soup at a friend's house, and I just had to get the recipe from her. I put my own twist on it, and made it Pesachdik. Don't be tempted to skip the step of searing the meat, because it really adds lots of flavor to the soup.

METHOD

1 Heat a large (8-quart) pot over medium-high heat. Sear flanken for approximately 5 minutes per side, or until the meat releases easily from the surface of the pot. Add all the vegetables.

2 Add water just to cover the vegetables; bring to a boil. Reduce the heat; simmer for 2 hours.

3 Remove flanken from soup. Remove meat from bones; discard bones. Set meat aside.

4 Use an immersion blender to process soup for a full 3 minutes, until smooth. Add salt and pepper to taste.

5 To serve, cut reserved flanken into chunks. Ladle soup into bowls; place a few pieces of flanken into each bowl.

Cook's Tip This recipe freezes amazingly well! Freeze pureed soup in an airtight container. Shred meat and freeze separately in a ziplock bag. Reheat meat in the oven before serving in the reheated soup.

Year 'Round When making this recipe during the year, see page 235 for non-Passover alternatives.

Meat and Cabbage Soup

meat – yields 10 servings – freezer friendly

INGREDIENTS

2 pounds flanken

2 (28-ounce) cans whole tomatoes with their liquid

1 (14-ounce) bag shredded cabbage, or **1 head** cabbage, shredded

1 Granny Smith apple, peeled and diced

¼ cup brown sugar

½ cup lemon juice

4 cups water

1 teaspoon kosher salt, or to taste

¼ teaspoon black pepper, or to taste

I'll eat stuffed cabbage in any shape or form, and this is a version of it in a soup. The apple in this recipe gives it a unique flavor and sweetness.

METHOD

1   In a large, heavy-bottomed pot, sear flanken on each side for 2-3 minutes, until meat releases from the pot.

2   Crush tomatoes lightly in your hand; then add the tomatoes and their liquid to the pot.

3   Add cabbage, apple, sugar, lemon juice, water, salt, and pepper.

4   Bring to a boil over high heat; reduce heat to low. Simmer for approximately 2 hours, until meat is tender.

5   Remove meat from soup. Discard bones; shred meat into bite-size pieces. Return to soup. Bring soup to a boil to reheat the meat.

6   Add additional salt and pepper to taste, if needed.

Kale, Apple, and Sausage Soup

meat – yields 8 servings – freezer friendly

INGREDIENTS

1 Tablespoon olive oil

1 large onion, diced

2 cloves garlic, crushed

1 large jalapeño pepper, seeded, ribs removed

3 stalks celery, diced

1 sweet potato, peeled and cubed

3 Gala apples, peeled and chopped

1 (6-ounce) package dried, cooked sausage, sliced into ½-inch rounds (see Cook's Tip, below)

1 bunch kale, chopped (about 6 cups), stems and center ribs removed

4 cups chicken or vegetable broth

1 (14.5 ounce) can diced tomatoes, with their liquid

½ teaspoon salt, or to taste

¼ teaspoon ground black pepper

dash sriracha (optional)

I call this my "blizzard soup," because I made it on a freezing-cold, snowy night to help warm my family. I couldn't get out to buy any ingredients, so I developed this recipe using whatever I had on hand. The resulting soup was such a hit — a real one-pot wonder!

METHOD

1 In a large (8-10-quart) soup pot, heat olive oil over medium-high heat. Add onion, garlic, jalapeño, celery, sweet potato, apples, and sausage. Sauté, stirring occasionally, until onion is translucent, 5-10 minutes.

2 Reduce heat to medium-low. Add kale; cover. Cook for 2 minutes.

3 Add broth, diced tomatoes with their liquid, salt, and pepper. Cover; cook for 15-20 minutes, until vegetables are tender.

4 Ladle soup into bowls. If using, add a dash of sriracha to each bowl just before serving.

Year 'Round When making this recipe during the year, see page 235 for non-Passover alternatives.

Cook's Tip Choose your favorite dried salami, cabanossi, or other sausage to add to the soup.

Watermelon Gazpacho

pareve – yields 6 servings

INGREDIENTS

½ **small** red onion

½ jalapeño pepper, seeds removed

3 cups chopped seedless watermelon, rind removed (about 1 pound watermelon flesh)

3 medium vine tomatoes, coarsely chopped

½ English hothouse cucumber, peeled and coarsely chopped

2 Tablespoons olive oil

2 Tablespoons red wine vinegar

1 teaspoon kosher salt

¼ teaspoon freshly ground black pepper

Don't be afraid because this soup is served cold. Gazpacho is light and perfect for a hot day. Gazpacho is traditionally made from raw tomatoes, but the sweetness of the watermelon is an amazing addition that makes this soup even more refreshing.

METHOD

1 In the bowl of a food processor fitted with the "S" blade or in a blender, puree the onion and jalapeño.

2 Add remaining ingredients; puree (some texture will remain).

3 Serve chilled.

Cook's Tip

For a dairy meal, sprinkle with crumbled feta cheese and sliced almonds.

Prepare Ahead

You can prepare the gazpacho 1 day in advance. Stir before serving, as components may separate.

Fish

Fish 'n Chips

pareve – yields 6-8 servings

INGREDIENTS

2 eggs, lightly beaten

2 Tablespoons white vinegar

1 cup potato starch

2 (6-ounce) bags potato sticks

2 pounds fresh baby flounder, cut into strips

• oil, for frying

• lemon wedges, for serving

• tartar sauce, for serving (see recipe, below)

Prepare Ahead

Coat the fish and freeze raw, between layers of parchment. Defrost; bake fresh.

Cook's Tip

Try various flavors of potato chips or potato sticks to change the flavor of this recipe.

Year 'Round

When making this recipe during the year, see page 235 for non-Passover alternatives.

Being an Australian, I couldn't resist including a fish 'n chips recipe. I came up with this playful twist, coating the fish in these iconic potato stick "chips." I love that this recipe is baked, not fried.

METHOD

1 Preheat oven to 350°F. Line a baking sheet with parchment paper; set aside.

2 Place eggs and vinegar into a bowl; whisk to combine. Place potato starch into a second bowl and potato sticks (not crushed) into a third.

3 Dip each piece of fish into potato starch, then into egg, and then into potato sticks, making sure the entire strip is fully coated. Place on prepared baking sheet.

4 Bake for 25 minutes.

5 Serve with a wedge of lemon and tartar sauce.

Tartar Sauce

INGREDIENTS

4 large canned Israeli pickles

1 cup mayonnaise

1 Tablespoon pickle juice

2 Tablespoons fresh lemon juice

METHOD

1 In a food processor fitted with the "S" blade, chop the pickles.

2 Add mayonnaise and pickle juice; pulse to combine.

Tangy Aioli Branzini

pareve – yields 6 servings

INGREDIENTS

6 (6-ounce) slices branzini

• salt

• pepper

½ cup mayonnaise

½ cup sweet chili sauce

When you're in a hurry and you need to make a really delicious fish meal really fast, this is the one for you! This aioli is also great with thinly cut chicken cutlets.

METHOD

1 Preheat oven to 350°F. Line a baking sheet with parchment paper.

2 Place branzini, skin-side down, on prepared baking sheet. Sprinkle with salt and pepper. Set aside.

3 In a small bowl, combine mayonnaise and sweet chili sauce. Generously spread the mixture on branzini.

4 Bake for 25 minutes, or until fish flakes easily when pierced in the center with a fork.

Cook's Tip

• This can also be made as a single-portion dish that can be ready in 5 minutes, for a quick and easy dinner. Use 1 tablespoon each mayonnaise and sweet chili sauce for a single portion. Microwave for 3- 5 minutes, depending on the power of the microwave.

• Instead of branzini, you can use salmon in this recipe.

Red Snapper en Papillote

pareve – yields 6 servings

INGREDIENTS

6 (4-ounce) red snapper fillets, with skin

2-3 cloves garlic, crushed

½ cup pitted and chopped Kalamata olives (optional)

½ cup grape tomatoes, halved

3 Tablespoons fresh parsley, chopped

• zest of **2** lemons

• salt, to taste

• pepper, to taste

This dish has a really beautiful presentation. Each guest gets a little "present" to open and enjoy as the fish course. "En papillote," literally "in parchment," is the French term indicating that a food is steamed while wrapped in parchment paper.

METHOD

1. Preheat the oven to 400°F. Prepare a baking sheet and 6 rectangular pieces of parchment paper, each long enough and wide enough to wrap each piece of fish completely.

2. Place 1 fillet, skin-side down, in the center of each piece of parchment; sprinkle with garlic and olives, if using. Top each with tomatoes, parsley, and lemon zest.

3. Season with salt and pepper to taste.

4. Fold the parchment around the fish, crimping the edges together to form an airtight package.

5. Place the parchment packets on prepared baking sheet; bake for 15-20 minutes, or until the parchment puffs.

6. To serve, transfer packets to plates; open carefully to avoid the steam. Fish should flake easily when pierced with a fork.

Prepare Ahead

Use salmon instead of red snapper. Bake for 20 minutes.

Cook's Tip

This really should be served on the day you make it. For best make-ahead results, prepare the packets in the morning and keep them in the fridge; bake them just before serving.

Crispy Flounder
with Pickled Onions

pareve – yields 6-8 servings – freezer friendly – gebrochts or non-gebrochts –

INGREDIENTS

1 cup potato starch

3 eggs, lightly beaten

1½ cups matzah meal, Pesach panko crumbs, or non-gebrochts crumbs

1 Tablespoon chili powder

1 teaspoon garlic powder

1 teaspoon onion powder

½ teaspoon kosher salt

⅛ teaspoon black pepper

2 pounds flounder, salmon or tilapia fillets, cut thin strips

• oil, for frying

Lighten Up

Instead of frying, spray fish with nonstick cooking spray; bake on a parchment paper-lined baking sheet at 400°F for 25 minutes.

Prepare Ahead

Freeze cooked fillets between layers of parchment paper. Onions can be prepared up to 1 week ahead.

My family loves to have "Taco Tuesday" night, and this fish is a favorite filling. On Pesach, we can't have taco shells, but we still enjoy this crispy fish topped with scrumptious pickled onions. You can serve it on a piece of matzah to replace the taco shell.

METHOD

1 **Set up a breading station:** Place potato starch into a shallow dish. Place eggs into a second shallow dish. Combine the panko crumbs and spices in a third shallow dish.

2 Dredge each piece of fish in the potato starch, then eggs, then crumbs, coating it well.

3 Set coated fish on a platter in a single layer until ready to fry.

4 Heat approximately ¼-inch of oil in a large pan over medium-high heat.

5 Working in batches, add the fish to the pan and fry until the coating is crispy and fish is cooked through, 2-3 minutes per side. Do not crowd pan. Drain on paper towels; transfer to a serving platter. Top with pickled red onions.

Pickled Red Onions

INGREDIENTS

2 large red onions, halved and thinly sliced

1 cup apple cider vinegar

3 Tablespoons sugar

1 heaping teaspoon kosher salt

METHOD

1 Combine all ingredients in a small pot. Bring to a boil over medium-high heat. Cook for 2 minutes.

2 Set aside to cool; serve over fried fish.

Cook's
Tip

Add guacamole
(page 30) and/or salsa
verde (page 42) to round
out your meal.

Pistachio-Crusted Salmon

pareve – yields 6-8 servings

All over the world, people stop me to tell me how much they love this quick, easy, and incredibly delicious recipe that I developed for my blog. The salty nuts, the sweetness of the sugar, and the kick of the horseradish make this recipe a perfect combination.

INGREDIENTS

¼ **cup** red horseradish (chrein)

¼ **cup** mayonnaise

1 (about 2-pound) whole side salmon, or **6-8** slices

1 cup shelled salted pistachios

½ **cup** brown sugar

2 Tablespoons lemon juice

METHOD

1 Preheat oven to 350°F. Line a baking sheet with parchment paper; set aside.

2 Mix the horseradish and mayonnaise together in a small bowl.

3 Place the salmon on prepared baking sheet; spread with horseradish mixture. Set aside.

4 In a food processor fitted with the "S" blade, chop the nuts until they are coarsely ground but not too fine. Add the brown sugar and lemon juice; pulse until the mixture looks like wet sand.

5 Pat nut mixture onto salmon, covering the entire surface.

6 Bake for 25 minutes, until the center flakes when pierced with a fork.

Prepare Ahead

Prepare the recipe through Step 5; then freeze. Fully defrost overnight in the fridge before baking.

Moroccan Salmon

pareve – yields 8 servings – freezer friendly

INGREDIENTS

2 Tablespoons olive oil

1 large onion, diced

1½ teaspoons cumin

8 (6-ounce) slices salmon

Sauce

¼ teaspoon cayenne pepper

3 cloves garlic, crushed

2 Tablespoons fresh parsley or cilantro, chopped

1 plum tomato, diced

1 (14-ounce) can tomato sauce

1 teaspoon kosher salt

½ cup water, if needed

The first time I ever had Moroccan salmon was at a henna party for a friend, and it became an instant favorite of mine. I put my own twist on it, and I've been making it ever since.

METHOD

1 Heat oil in a large sauté pan over medium heat. Add onion; sauté until translucent, approximately 8 minutes. Reduce heat to low. Add cumin; sauté for additional 3 minutes.

2 Place fish fillets on the onion mixture. Cook for 3 minutes; turn to coat other side and cook for additional 3 minutes.

3 **Prepare the sauce:** In a small bowl, mix cayenne pepper, garlic, parsley, tomato, tomato sauce, and salt. Pour mixture over fish. Add water to cover fish (approximately ½ cup), if necessary. Cook, uncovered, on low for an additional 15 minutes.

Cook's Tip

• You can replace the salmon with white fish, flounder, or tilapia.

• Instead of cooking this on the stovetop, place the seasoned sautéed onion into a 9 x 13-inch pan, top with salmon, and add the sauce. Cover; bake at 350°F for about 25 minutes.

Year 'Round

When making this recipe during the year, see page 235 for non-Passover alternatives.

Gravlax

pareve — yields 12-14 servings per side — freezer friendly

My dad, Jack Stein, made this Norwegian salmon dish for every special holiday. Now it has become a favorite in my house as well — some of my friends will come over only if I promise to serve it! Make sure to plan ahead, because it needs two days to cure in the fridge.

INGREDIENTS

2 (2-pound) whole sides salmon
4 Tablespoons salt
4 Tablespoons sugar
2 Tablespoon white pepper
1 large bunch dill

METHOD

1 Place the two sides of salmon, skin-side down, onto a large baking sheet.

2 In a small bowl, mix together salt, sugar, and pepper. Sprinkle over salmon, thickly coating the surface.

3 Place dill over spices, covering the salmon.

4 Place fish sides, one on top of the other, skin-side out, so the flesh sides are touching.

5 Tightly wrap salmon in heavy-duty foil. Return salmon to the baking sheet; place heavy weights, such as canned vegetables, on the salmon to weigh it down.

6 Place baking sheet with the cans into the refrigerator. After 24 hours, turn the salmon over; replace cans and return all to the fridge for an additional 24 hours.

7 Remove dill and excess spices; thinly slice salmon on an angle. Serve with Dill Sauce, below, if desired.

Cook's Tip

• It's easiest to slice the salmon while slightly frozen; you'll be able to get thinner slices that way.

• I like to serve this with a Late Harvest Riesling.

Prepare Ahead

Remove dill after 48 hours. At that point, wrap the salmon well and freeze it. Slice just before serving.

Dill Sauce

INGREDIENTS

1 cup mayonnaise
½ cup dill, finely chopped
2 Tablespoons lemon juice
¼ teaspoon salt

METHOD

› Combine all ingredients in a small bowl. Stir well to combine. Serve alongside gravlax.

Sweet & Sour Tilapia

pareve – yields 8 servings – freezer friendly

INGREDIENTS

1-2 pounds tilapia fillets, each cut in half lengthwise

1 teaspoon kosher salt

¼ teaspoon black pepper

Sauce

3 Tablespoons oil

1 large onion, diced

2 cloves garlic, crushed

4 carrots, peeled and sliced into rounds

1 cup ketchup

¾ cup brown sugar

pinch cinnamon

1 cup water

1 (14-ounce) can pineapple chunks, with their liquid

• salt, to taste

• pepper, to taste

When I started developing recipes and giving cooking classes, this recipe was the first collaboration with my mother. My mum was visiting from Australia and we had a great time coming up with the recipe together. Ever since then, it's been one of the most frequently requested recipes from my catering clients.

METHOD

1 Preheat oven to 350°F. Prepare an ovenproof baking dish large enough to hold all the fillets in one layer.

2 Rinse fish; pat dry. Season with salt and pepper. Place into prepared baking dish; set aside.

3 **Prepare the sauce:** Heat oil in a large frying pan over medium heat. Sauté onions with garlic until soft. Add carrots; sauté for 2 minutes. Add ketchup, brown sugar, cinnamon, water, and pineapple chunks with their liquid.

4 Bring sauce to a boil; reduce heat and simmer for 5-10 minutes until the sauce thickens. Season with salt and pepper, to taste.

5 Pour sauce over fish in the baking dish. Bake for 20 minutes, until fish flakes easily when pierced with a fork.

Cook's Tip

Skinless salmon fillets also work well in this recipe. I have also used this sauce and technique with chicken cutlets and with boiled corn beef.

Quick Poached Salmon

pareve – yields 6 servings

INGREDIENTS

1 onion, sliced

1 cup sugar

½ cup vinegar

½ cup lemon juice

3½ cups water

1 Tablespoon kosher salt

4 bay leaves

6 (6-ounce) slices salmon

This was the first fish recipe I cooked after I got married. My friend served this fish when I went to her house for Friday night dinner and I asked her for the recipe. It's been more than 20 years and I'm still making it! Note that the longer this fish sits in the liquid, the more pronounced the flavor will be. If you like a strong pickled flavor, prepare it an extra day or two ahead of time.

METHOD

1 Heat a medium pot over medium-low heat. Add onion and sugar; cook together so the sugar dissolves in the liquid from the onion.

2 Add remaining ingredients; bring to a boil. Gently lower salmon into pot. Reduce heat to low; simmer, covered, for 20 minutes until cooked through.

3 Chill salmon in poaching liquid before serving; garnish with the onion slices.

Cook's Tip

Serve this fish with dill sauce (page 102), remoulade sauce (page 30), or tartar sauce (page 90).

Prepare Ahead

This salmon can be prepared up to two days ahead of time.

Poultry

Quinoa and Mushroom Stuffed Capons

meat – yields 8 servings – freezer friendly

Capons are attractive when served for a Yom Tov meal, and they make a great change from roasts and meat. In the kosher market, capon refers to a deboned chicken thigh with the skin on. The skin keeps the capons moist while cooking, and the filling becomes a built-in side dish.

INGREDIENTS

1 Tablespoon oil

1 large onion, diced

10-ounces white button mushrooms, finely diced

1 cups raw quinoa

2 cups water

1 teaspoon kosher salt

¼ teaspoon black pepper

8 chicken capons

Sauce

1 Tablespoon oil

1 large onion, finely diced

2 cloves garlic, crushed

¾ cup ketchup

¾ cup brown sugar

1 cup water

Year 'Round

When making this recipe during the year, see page 235 for non-Passover alternatives.

METHOD

1 **Prepare the stuffing:** Heat oil in a large frying pan over medium heat. Add onion; sauté until they start to brown. Add mushrooms; cook for an additional few minutes, until softened.

2 Add quinoa, water, salt, and pepper; bring to a boil. Reduce to a simmer; cook, covered, for approximately 15 minutes, until the liquid has been absorbed. Set aside to cool.

3 Preheat oven to 350°F. Prepare 1 (9x13-inch) baking pan.

4 Stuff each capon with quinoa mixture. Place stuffed capons into prepared pan. Place any remaining stuffing around the capons. Set aside.

5 **Prepare the sauce:** In a small pot, heat oil over medium heat. Add onion; fry until translucent. Add remaining sauce ingredients; bring to a boil.

6 Reduce heat to a simmer; cook for five minutes, until sauce has thickened slightly. Pour over capons in pan.

7 Cover pan tightly; bake for 1 hour. Uncover; bake for an additional 30 minutes, until the tops start to brown.

8 Serve with additional stuffing on the side.

Coke Chicken

The sugars in the Coke caramelize the chicken and onions in this dish so that they become dark, sweet, and delicious.

INGREDIENTS

2 medium onions, halved and sliced

8 chicken quarters (see Cook's Tip, below)

1 teaspoon salt

¼ teaspoon black pepper

1 Tablespoon garlic powder

Sauce

1 cup Coke

1 cup barbecue sauce

1 cup raspberry jam

METHOD

1 Preheat oven to 400°F.

2 Place sliced onions into a large pan. Place chicken over onions; season with salt, pepper, and garlic powder.

3 **Prepare the sauce:** In a medium bowl, combine Coke, barbecue sauce, and raspberry jam. Pour sauce over chicken.

4 Bake, uncovered, for 1 hour 15 minutes, basting after 40 minutes, until golden brown.

Cook's Tip

• Use your family's favorite chicken parts.

• Do not use Diet Coke, as the sugars in regular Coke are needed to caramelize the chicken.

Prepare Ahead

Prepare through Step 3; freeze before baking and bake it fresh after it has defrosted.

Sweet and Salty Pecan Chicken Cutlets

meat – yields 4-6 servings

INGREDIENTS

1½ pound chicken cutlets, cut into nugget or finger shapes

¼ cup potato starch

2 eggs

2½ teaspoons kosher salt, divided

1 Tablespoon pure maple syrup

2 cups finely chopped pecans (see Cook's Tip, below)

¼ cup sugar

• oil, for frying

This is a great change-up from a traditional breaded chicken cutlet. The sweet flavors of the sugar and maple syrup are perfect together with the salty nuts.

METHOD

1 Place chicken pieces into a medium bowl; toss with potato starch until all chicken is coated.

2 Place eggs, 1 teaspoon salt, and maple syrup into a second bowl; whisk to combine.

3 Combine pecans, sugar, and remaining 1½ teaspoons salt in a third bowl; stir to combine.

4 Dredge each piece of chicken in the egg mixture, then in the pecan mixture.

5 Heat oil in a large frying pan over medium heat. Fry each piece of chicken for 3-5 minutes per side, until golden brown and cooked through. Don't overcrowd pan while frying.

6 Serve with Creamy Dipping Sauce (see page 184), if desired.

Prepare Ahead
You can freeze these after frying, but for best results, freeze them raw. Defrost and fry just before serving.

Cook's Tip

• If you can't find maple syrup, use honey instead.

• For best results, crush the pecans in the food processor or with a big knife. You want them to be finely chopped, but still have some texture. Don't chop until they are fine crumbs.

Braised Chicken
with Apples and Sweet Potatoes

meat – yields 4-6 servings – freezer friendly

This recipe was given to me by my photographer, Miriam Pascal. The recipe was shared on her blog, where it has become a favorite of thousands of readers. When I tasted this recipe, I knew why it was such a hit. There's a hint of sweetness, the chicken is incredibly soft, and the vegetables it cooks in make a wonderful side dish.

INGREDIENTS

2 Tablespoons olive oil

4-6 chicken bottoms

3 large onions (I use Spanish), finely diced

3 medium sweet potatoes, peeled and finely diced

2 large carrots, peeled and finely diced

3 medium apples, peeled and finely diced

⅔ cup chicken or vegetable broth

2-4 Tablespoons honey, to taste

2 teaspoons kosher salt, or to taste

1 teaspoon ground cinnamon

⅛-¼ teaspoon cayenne pepper

METHOD

1 In a large, heavy-bottomed pot, heat oil over medium-high heat. Brown the chicken on each side for approximately 2 minutes, until slightly browned. Remove from pot; set aside.

2 Without scraping or washing pot, add onions; sauté over medium heat for approximately 5 minutes, until translucent.

3 Add remaining vegetables and apples; sauté for an additional 5-10 minutes, stirring occasionally.

4 Add broth, honey, salt, cinnamon, and cayenne pepper. Stir to combine.

5 Add browned chicken to the vegetable/apple mixture, covering chicken completely. Bring mixture to a boil; reduce heat to low. Cover; simmer for 2 hours. For a thicker sauce, uncover the pot, turn the heat up to medium high, and let the liquids reduce for a few minutes. Serve hot.

Cook's Tip

• Serve this with mashed potatoes to soak up the delicious gravy.

• Apples such as Gala, Fuji, or other sweet, juicy varieties all work well in this recipe.

Chicken Piccata

meat — yields 6 servings — freezer friendly

Lemon is my favorite flavor, and it really comes through in this traditional chicken dish.

INGREDIENTS

6 chicken cutlets, pounded thin

juice of **2** lemons (about ½ cup)

1 cup potato starch

¼ teaspoon kosher salt

pinch ground black pepper

2 Tablespoons olive oil

2 Tablespoons oil

Sauce

1 cup chicken stock or white wine

½ cup lemon juice

½ teaspoon kosher salt

2 Tablespoons fresh chopped parsley leaves, for garnish

METHOD

1   Place chicken and lemon juice into a small bowl; marinate for five minutes. Drain the chicken; set aside. Discard the marinade.

2   In a small bowl, stir together potato starch, salt, and pepper. Dredge each piece of chicken in the potato starch mixture until well coated.

3   Heat oils in a large skillet over medium high heat. Add half the chicken pieces; do not crowd the pan. Brown well on each side, approximately 3 minutes per side. Remove chicken from the pan; set aside. Repeat with remaining chicken.

4   **Prepare the sauce:** Add chicken stock, lemon juice, and salt to skillet. Use a spatula to scrape up the browned bits. Return chicken to the pan. Simmer the sauce for a few minutes until it reduces and thickens.

5   Sprinkle parsley over chicken before serving.

Cook's Tip

• When using white wine to make this recipe (as pictured), the chicken will be a more vivid color than when using chicken stock.

• We use two types of oil in this recipe because olive oil may burn when used alone at this frying temperature.

Zucchini Stuffed Chicken

meat – yields 8 servings – freezer friendly

This dish presents beautifully, with the secret zucchini hiding under the skin.

INGREDIENTS

2 whole chickens, cut into quarters

1 Tablespoon oil

1 medium onion, diced

2 medium zucchini, grated

2 teaspoons kosher salt, divided

1 teaspoon potato starch

2 Tablespoons honey

Prepare Ahead

Prepare the chicken with the stuffing; freeze before baking. Defrost and bake just before serving.

METHOD

1 Preheat oven to 400°F. Divide chicken between 2 (9x13-inch) pans; set aside.

2 **Prepare the stuffing:** Heat oil over medium heat in a large frying pan. Add onion; sauté approximately 5 minutes, until softened.

3 Add zucchini and 1 teaspoon salt. Cook an additional 10 minutes, until some of the liquid cooks off and the zucchini has softened. Sprinkle in potato starch; stir well until starch has been mixed in and dissolved. Remove from heat; set aside to cool.

4 Use your fingers to gently loosen the chicken skin. Stuff approximately 2 tablespoons of stuffing under the skin of each piece.

5 Sprinkle remaining salt over the chicken; drizzle with honey. Gently spread drizzled honey over the chicken.

6 Bake, uncovered, for 1 hour 15 minutes, basting with pan juices halfway through.

Tequila Lime Chicken

meat – yields 6 servings

This fresh chicken recipe is bursting with bold flavors.

INGREDIENTS

Marinade

¼ cup tequila, optional

juice of **4** limes (about ½ cup)

2 Tablespoons oil

1 teaspoon lime zest

1 jalapeño pepper, seeded, finely diced

2 cloves garlic, crushed

¼ cup parsley or cilantro, finely chopped

1 teaspoon kosher salt

¼ teaspoon black pepper

2-3 pounds boneless and skinless chicken breasts

METHOD

1 Preheat oven to 400°F. Line a baking sheet with parchment paper; set aside.

2 **Prepare the marinade:** Place all marinade ingredients into a bowl; whisk to combine.

3 Add chicken; marinate for 10-15 minutes (no longer, or the acidic lime juice will turn the chicken white.)

4 Spread chicken in a single layer on prepared baking sheet. Bake for 20 minutes, until cooked through.

Hawaiian Pargiyot

meat – yields 6 servings

This recipe comes from my foodie friend, the teenage chef Eitan Bernath, who made it at a Pesach program where he served his version of this dish to hundreds of guests.

INGREDIENTS

Marinade

½ cup pineapple juice

½ cup imitation soy sauce

1 Tablespoon honey

2 Tablespoons oil

1 Tablespoon brown sugar

2 cloves garlic, crushed

1 teaspoon ground ginger

½ teaspoon salt

2-3 pounds dark chicken cutlets (pargiyot), pounded or cut thin

METHOD

1 **Prepare the marinade:** Place all marinade ingredients into a bowl; whisk to combine.

2 Add chicken; marinate in the fridge for about 1 hour.

3 Preheat oven to 400°F. Line a baking sheet with parchment paper.

4 Remove chicken from marinade; place in a single layer on prepared baking sheet. Discard any remaining marinade.

5 Bake for about 25 minutes, until cooked through.

Cook's Tip

- You can puree the marinade in the food processor for an extra-smooth marinade. You can also make this recipe using salmon.

- This can also be made on a barbecue or grill pan on the stovetop.

Cook's Tip

Turn these into beautiful kebobs: Cut the chicken into chunks and thread onto skewers. Thread pieces of pepper, pineapple chunks, and red onion between each piece of chicken.

Prepare Ahead

Place the chicken and marinade into a ziplock bag and freeze. Defrost and bake fresh.

Citrus-Glazed Duck Breasts

meat – yields 4 servings

INGREDIENTS

2 duck breasts

• kosher salt, to taste

• pepper, to taste

Glaze

juice of **1** orange (about 2 Tablespoons)

1 Tablespoon fresh lime juice (from ½ lime)

1 teaspoon orange zest

1 teaspoon lime zest

1 Tablespoon sugar

2 Tablespoons Pesach vodka

1 teaspoon potato starch

3 Tablespoons water

When I was growing up in Australia, duck was a huge delicacy and had to be custom ordered for special occasions. My dad loves duck, and I developed this recipe to serve when he came to my house for Yom Tov.

METHOD

1 **Prepare the duck breasts:** Slice the duck breasts lengthwise into 2 equal halves; score the skin in a cross-hatch pattern without cutting through the flesh. Sprinkle with salt and pepper.

2 Place duck breasts, skin-side down, into a cold sauté pan, then turn the heat to medium (this will help the fat render out). Fry each duck breast over medium heat until golden brown, 5-7 minutes. Skin should be crispy and brown. Flip duck to the second side; fry for 3-4 minutes. The optimal internal temperature is 130°F. Set aside to rest.

3 **Meanwhile, prepare the glaze:** In a small saucepan over low heat, combine orange juice, lime juice, zests, sugar, and vodka. Cook, stirring constantly, until the sugar has dissolved, approximately 2 minutes.

4 In a small bowl, combine potato starch and water; stir until smooth. Add to juice mixture; stir to combine. Bring to a boil, stirring constantly, until glaze thickens.

5 Once duck has rested, slice on the diagonal and plate. Pour thickened glaze over duck slices; serve immediately.

Cook's Tip

If you can't find Pesach vodka, use white wine or orange liqueur instead.

White Wine and Herb Roasted Turkey Roll

meat – yields 8-10 servings – freezer friendly

If you're looking for a lighter alternative to meat, turkey roast is the way to go!

INGREDIENTS

1 Granny Smith apple, with peel, sliced into half-moons

1 medium onion, halved, and sliced

1 (3-4-pound) rolled turkey roast in the net

2 Tablespoons olive oil

4-5 cloves garlic, crushed

¼ teaspoon dried thyme

1 teaspoon paprika

1 teaspoon kosher salt

¼ teaspoon black pepper

1 cup semi-dry white wine

METHOD

1 Preheat oven to 350°F.

2 Place apples and onion into a roasting pan. Place turkey roast on them. Set aside.

3 In a small bowl, combine olive oil, garlic, thyme, paprika, salt, and black pepper to make a paste. Rub the mixture over the entire surface of the turkey.

4 Add the wine into the pan, around the roast. Don't pour it directly over the turkey, or the paste will be washed off.

5 Cover the turkey; roast for 1 hour 15 minutes until a meat thermometer inserted into the thickest part registers 155°F.

6 Let roast rest before slicing cold. Reheat gently in pan juices over low heat.

Prepare Ahead

If you plan to freeze the roast, seal the pan juices and turkey in a ziplock bag, squeezing out the air. Defrost and slice before gently reheating.

Cook's Tip

• Be careful not to overcook your turkey roll, or it will be dry. Using a meat thermometer ensures that you cook this roast just right.

• Leftovers can be tossed into a salad or used in the Cauliflower Fried "Rice" (page 192).

Cranberry Glazed Turkey and Spinach Meatloaf

meat – yields 8-10 servings – freezer friendly

I developed this recipe right before Thanksgiving, when I saw a big display of cranberry sauce on the shelf in the grocery store. It was right then and there that the idea for this amazing meatloaf started to take shape in my mind.

INGREDIENTS

Cranberry Glaze

1 (14-ounce) can whole berry cranberry sauce

½ cup ketchup

½ cup brown sugar

1 Tablespoon balsamic vinegar

Meatloaf

1 Tablespoon oil

1 medium onion, peeled and diced

12 ounces frozen spinach, defrosted and squeezed dry

2 pounds ground turkey

2 eggs

1 teaspoon kosher salt

¼ teaspoon black pepper

2 Tablespoons ketchup

Cook's Tip

• Make mini meatloaves as an appetizer: Divide the mixture into muffin pans instead of loaf pans; glaze and bake for 20 minutes. This will yield about 18 appetizer portions.

• You can use this cranberry glaze on a corned beef. You can also use it as a dipping sauce alongside the meatloaf.

METHOD

1 **Prepare the cranberry glaze:** Place all sauce ingredients into a small pot; stir to combine. Bring to a boil; cook for a few minutes. Set aside.

2 **Prepare the meatloaf:** Preheat oven to 350°F. Prepare 2 (1-pound) loaf pans (each 3.5 x 6 inches).

3 Heat oil in a large frying pan over medium heat. Add onion; cook, stirring occasionally, for approximately 5 minutes, until softened.

4 Add spinach; cook, stirring occasionally, until any liquid cooks off, approximately 10 minutes.

5 Remove from heat; cool for a few minutes. Add turkey, eggs, salt, pepper, ketchup, and ½ cup prepared cranberry glaze.

6 Divide the mixture between two loaf pans; top with remaining cranberry glaze, dividing evenly.

7 Bake for 50 minutes, uncovered, until cooked through.

8 After baking, pour off any excess liquid that has accumulated around the sides.

Winner Winner
Chicken Dinner

meat – yields 8 servings – freezer friendly

The name says it all! This is a winning dish for everyone in the family — and especially for the cook, because it's so easy to prepare!

INGREDIENTS

2 whole chickens, cut into quarters

1 teaspoon kosher salt

1 cup salsa

1 cup orange jam

1 (11-ounce) can mandarin orange pieces, drained

METHOD

1 Preheat oven to 400°F. Prepare roasting pan large enough to hold the chicken snuggly.

2 Place chicken into prepared pan; season with salt.

3 In a medium mixing bowl, stir together salsa, orange jam, and mandarin oranges. Pour over chicken.

4 Bake, uncovered, for 1 hour 15 minutes, basting after 40 minutes.

Prepare Ahead

Freeze raw chicken in sauce. Defrost in fridge; bake the day of serving.

Meat

Herb-Crusted Lamb Chops

pareve – yields 8 servings

INGREDIENTS

2 Tablespoons fresh chopped parsley

2 Tablespoons fresh chopped mint

2 Tablespoons fresh chopped rosemary

1 Tablespoon extra-virgin olive oil

1 Tablespoon prepared white horseradish

½ teaspoon kosher salt

¼ teaspoon black pepper

12 lamb chops, frenched (see Cook's Tip below)

Lamb is a very popular Australian meat, so it's fitting that these lamb chops have become one of my most famous dishes. I make this recipe for special occasions, such as Yamim Tovim, anniversaries, and birthdays.

METHOD

1 Preheat the oven to 400°F. Line a baking sheet with parchment paper; set aside.

2 In a food processor fitted with the "S" blade, pulse parsley, mint, and rosemary until coarsely chopped. Add olive oil and horseradish; process until the mixture forms a paste, approximately 30 seconds. Transfer mixture to a bowl; season with salt and pepper, mixing well to combine.

3 Place lamb chops on prepared baking sheet. Spread a spoonful of the herb mixture evenly over each chop.

4 Bake until the crust is golden and crisp and the lamb is pink inside (lamb is always served on the rare side), 5-7 minutes. Serve warm.

Prepare Ahead
Prepare the chops; freeze before cooking. Defrost in fridge; cook fresh.

Cook's Tip
• You can spread this crust on a 4-pound lamb roast. For rare, bake at 400°F until roast reaches an internal temperature of 120°F.

• "Frenched" means that the meat has been cut away from the end of the bone.

Maple Glazed
Rack of Ribs

meat – yields 6 servings – freezer friendly

INGREDIENTS

1 (4-5-pound) rack beef ribs

1 Tablespoon extra-virgin olive oil

1 teaspoon kosher salt

¼ teaspoon black pepper

1 teaspoon paprika

1 teaspoon onion powder

6 cloves garlic, crushed

1 Tablespoon brown sugar

½ cup pure maple syrup

½ cup white wine

2 Tablespoons apple cider vinegar

2 Tablespoons tomato paste

1 teaspoon kosher salt

I have made this as a cholent alternative for Shabbat lunch. It's quick and easy to prepare, and then you can just forget about it until you wake up to the amazing aroma of slow-cooked ribs.

METHOD

1   Preheat oven to 200°F. Place ribs into a large roasting pan; set aside.

2   In a small bowl, combine oil, salt, pepper, paprika, onion powder, garlic, and sugar. Mix well to form a paste. Rub paste all over the top and bottom of the meat.

3   If you have time, let the meat stand at room temperature for 1 hour to absorb some of the flavors.

4   In a second bowl, mix maple syrup, wine, vinegar, tomato paste, and salt. Pour over the meat. Cover the meat really well. Place in the oven for 16 hours or overnight.

5   Brush pan juices over meat; cut apart ribs just before serving.

When making this recipe during the year, see page 235 for non-Passover alternatives.

Herb-Grilled London Broil

meat – yields 4-6 servings

INGREDIENTS

2½ pounds thick-cut shoulder London broil

½ cup olive oil

1 Tablespoon balsamic vinegar

3 sprigs chopped fresh rosemary

1 Tablespoon chopped fresh thyme

1 teaspoon salt

¼ teaspoon black pepper

6 cloves garlic, crushed

Rosemary and steak are a classic pairing that really makes this London broil shine. This is delicious when served at room temperature, which makes it perfect if your oven isn't on for Yom Tov or Shabbat. Be sure to take it out of the fridge an hour or so before serving to allow the meat to come to room temperature.

METHOD

1 Place all ingredients in a shallow dish or a ziplock bag. Cover or seal the container. Marinate in the refrigerator for a few hours, up to overnight.

2 Remove meat from fridge; allow it to come to room temperature before grilling.

3 Preheat broiler. Broil meat for 8 minutes per side, then turn off the heat. Let meat remain in the oven for approximately 10 minutes, or until meat reaches your desired level of doneness (see Cook's Tip, below).

4 Cut across the grain into thin slices before serving.

Cook's Tip

The length of time this meat needs in the oven depends on the thickness of the steak as well as how well done you like it. For a thinner piece of meat, leave it in the turned-off oven for less time. If you like your meat medium or well done, leave it in longer. The instructions above will result in rare to medium-rare London broil.

Veal Roast
with Mushroom Sauce

meat – yields 12 servings – freezer friendly

Veal has always been regarded in my family as special-occasion meat that I make only on Yom Tov. The beauty of this recipe is that the sauce cooks along with the meat, saving you from an extra step. The savory roast paired with the flavorful mushrooms make this a winning dish.

INGREDIENTS

1 (4-5-pound) boneless veal roast

4 cloves garlic, crushed

1 teaspoon kosher salt

¼ teaspoon black pepper

1 Tablespoon oil

½ cup dry white wine, divided

1 large onion, chopped

16 ounces cremini or baby bella mushrooms, sliced

1 Tablespoon fresh rosemary, chopped

1 teaspoon fresh thyme

1 teaspoon kosher salt

Cook's Tip

• Always slice a roast after it has properly cooled. I put mine in the fridge for several hours, which helps me get nice, even slices. Reheat in sauce, covered, over low temperature so the meat doesn't dry out.

• If you can't find cremini mushrooms, use white button mushrooms instead.

METHOD

1 Preheat the oven to 350°F. Prepare a roasting pan large enough to hold the roast.

2 Rub garlic, salt, and pepper all over the roast, coating all sides.

3 Heat oil in a large skillet over medium-high heat. Sear roast for approximately a minute (or less) per side, until it starts to brown. Remove roast from skillet; place it into prepared roasting pan.

4 **Prepare the mushroom sauce:** Reduce heat to medium; add a tablespoon of wine to the skillet. Deglaze the pan by stirring and scraping the bottom of the pan to loosen all the meat drippings. (This will add lots of flavor to the sauce.)

5 Add onion; cook for a few minutes, until onion starts to brown. Add mushrooms, rosemary, thyme, and salt. Cook for 7-10 minutes, until the mushrooms have softened. Add remaining wine; then pour sauce over roast in pan.

6 Cover; bake for approximately 1 hour 30 minutes, until a thermometer inserted into the thickest part of the roast reaches 140°F for medium rare, 155°F for medium, or 165°F for well done.

Red Wine Shoulder Roast

meat – yields 10 servings – freezer friendly

INGREDIENTS

1 (5-pound) shoulder roast

2 large onions, sliced

1 Tablespoon extra-virgin olive oil

6 cloves garlic, crushed

1 teaspoon kosher salt

½ teaspoon black pepper

1 teaspoon paprika

1 teaspoon onion powder

1 cup red wine

1 cup ketchup

This is our "Friday-night" roast — everyone looks forward to how juicy and delicious it is. Using a meat thermometer takes the guesswork out of cooking this roast, and will ensure that the meat is perfectly cooked. My family prefers it rare, but you can cook it longer if you prefer your meat more well-done.

METHOD

1 Preheat oven to 400°F.

2 Place onions into a roasting pan. Place meat atop onions.

3 In a small bowl, combine oil, garlic, salt, and spices, mixing them together to form a paste.

4 Rub the paste all over the meat.

5 In a separate bowl, combine wine and ketchup; pour mixture over meat. Place pan into oven.

6 Bake at 400°F, uncovered, for 20 minutes to brown the meat. Then reduce the oven temperature to 350°F. Cover the meat; cook until the internal temperature reaches 130°F, approximately 1 hour 30 minutes for medium.

7 Remove from oven. Allow roast to cool, then slice it. Pour pan juices over meat to serve.

Prepare Ahead

To freeze and reheat, slice the meat and pour all pan juices over it. Wrap it really well and freeze it. When ready to serve, defrost overnight in the fridge; then gently heat it at 200-250°F, until warmed through.

Cook's Tip

I like to use a probe to make sure I get perfectly cooked meat. It takes out the guesswork of when the meat is ready. If you don't have a probe, stick a long toothpick or skewer into the roast. The juices should run clear. The ideal way to eat this roast is medium to medium-rare.

Spiced Braised Flanken

meat – yields 10-12 servings – freezer friendly

INGREDIENTS

Spice rub

6 strips flanken

3 Tablespoons brown sugar

2 Tablespoons cumin

1 Tablespoon garlic powder

1 teaspoon paprika

1½ teaspoons cinnamon

1 teaspoon rosemary

½ teaspoon salt

½ teaspoon black pepper

Sauce

2 cups barbecue sauce

1 cup red dry wine

This recipe is magnificent! Braising is a cooking process that involves searing the meat (or chicken) over high heat, then adding liquid and cooking it low and slow. The result is meat that's incredibly tender and so delicious. The spice rub on the meat really adds an extra layer of incredible flavor.

METHOD

1 Place meat into a large roasting pan; set aside. Heat a broiler or grill pan.

2 **Prepare the spice rub:** In a small bowl, combine brown sugar, cumin, garlic powder, paprika, cinnamon, rosemary, salt, and pepper. Rub over all surfaces of the flanken.

3 Broil or grill flanken on high for 2-3 minutes per side; set aside.

4 Preheat the oven to 325°F.

5 **Prepare the sauce:** Whisk together barbecue sauce and wine until smooth. Pour sauce over broiled flanken.

6 Cover pan tightly; bake for 3 hours.

Cook's Tip

• Don't skip the broiling stage; it really boosts the flavor!

• Double the spice rub and keep it in an airtight container in the freezer. You'll find yourself making this recipe over and over!

Seder Pot Roast

meat – yields 8 servings – freezer friendly

INGREDIENTS

1 Tablespoon oil

1 (4-pound) California roast

2 Tablespoons potato starch

1 large onion, quartered

2 large loose carrots, peel and cut into chunks

1 teaspoon kosher salt

1 Tablespoon fish-free imitation Worcestershire sauce

2 cloves garlic, crushed

1 cup red wine

½ cup ketchup

¼ cup barbecue sauce

It's traditional that on the night of the Seder we do not eat meat that has been roasted in the oven, so I developed this stovetop meat dish for my Pesach catering clients to serve instead. The recipe is also ideal for Yom Tov, if your oven is off and you want a freshly cooked main dish.

METHOD

1 Heat oil over high heat in a large pot or Dutch oven.

2 Dredge the roast on all sides in potato starch. Sear in the hot oil for 1-2 minutes per side, until meat is well-browned. Add onion and carrots to the pot.

3 In a small bowl, mix together remaining ingredients; pour over meat. Bring to a boil, then reduce heat to low. Cover tightly; simmer for 3 hours, until the meat is tender.

4 Let roast rest before slicing cold. Reheat gently, over low heat.

Cook's Tip

French roast or brisket also work well in this recipe.

Prepare Ahead

Slice roast before freezing.

Sweet and Savory Brisket

meat – yields about 12 servings – freezer friendly

INGREDIENTS

3 onions, sliced

8 cloves garlic, crushed

1 teaspoon dried basil

1 Tablespoon paprika

1 teaspoon kosher salt

2 Tablespoons olive oil

2 Tablespoons oil

1 (4-pound) brisket

½ cup apricot jam

½ cup red wine

2 Tablespoons lemon juice

You can't have a Pesach cookbook without a great brisket recipe! This amazing brisket is so good, you'll even love the leftovers — the longer the brisket sits in the cooking liquid, the more flavorful it gets.

METHOD

1 Place onion slices into a large roasting pan. Set aside.

2 In a small bowl, combine garlic, basil, paprika, salt and olive oil to make a paste. Rub mixture all over brisket.

3 In a large sauté pan, heat 2 tablespoons oil. Sear brisket on both sides, approximately 4 minutes on each side. Place brisket over onions in roasting pan.

4 In a small bowl, combine jam, wine, and lemon juice. Pour over brisket and onions. Marinate for 1 hour in the refrigerator.

5 Preheat oven to 325°F. Roast brisket, covered, for 3 hours.

6 Cool; slice against the grain and serve.

Prepare Ahead

For freezing instructions see Prepare Ahead note on page 138.

Cook's Tip

Even though first cut brisket is considered by many to be of higher quality, I prefer second cut, which has more marbling, yielding a juicier and softer roast.

Ultimate Pesach Cholent

INGREDIENTS

Kishka

1 carrot, peeled

1 potato, peeled

1 stalk celery

1 small onion

⅓ cup oil

5 Tablespoons potato starch

1 cup matzah ball mix or non-gebrochts matzah ball mix

1 teaspoon salt

1½ teaspoons paprika

Cholent

1 Tablespoon kosher salt

1 Tablespoon paprika

1 Tablespoon garlic powder

6 russet or Idaho potatoes, peeled and cut into ½-inch dice

2 sweet potatoes, peeled and quartered

2 onions, quartered

2 pounds bone-in flanken

2 Tablespoons potato starch

3 cups water

1 cup ketchup

½ cup red wine

In order to make the "ultimate" Pesach cholent, I tried numerous versions over weeks and weeks, but wasn't so happy with the results. I mentioned my struggles to my friend Miriam, and she told me that her father, Harry Pascal, makes the most amazing Pesach cholent. His secret? He cuts potatoes into little pieces to give the cholent that bean-like texture. I tried that, and finally did have the **ultimate** *Pesach cholent. Don't skip the kishka in this recipe, because it really takes the cholent to the next level.*

METHOD

1 **Prepare the kishka:** In the bowl of a food processor fitted with the "S" blade, puree the vegetables.

2 Add remaining ingredients; mix to combine.

3 Place the mixture in a rectangular piece of parchment paper. Roll up tightly, making sure both ends are closed, to ensure that it doesn't leak while cooking. Set aside.

4 **Prepare the cholent:** In a small bowl, combine salt, paprika, and garlic powder. Set aside.

5 In a medium bowl, toss potatoes, sweet potatoes, onions, and flanken with the spice mixture. Place into a slow cooker.

6 In a small bowl, dissolve potato starch in the water. Add ketchup and wine. Add to slow cooker. Place prepared kishka into cholent.

7 Cook on low until ready to serve, 12 hours or overnight, until flanken is tender.

Cook's Tip

Make really flavorful matzah balls by using this kishka mixture. Form balls of kishka mixture and boil in salted water or chicken soup.

Coffee Infused Chili

meat – yields 6 servings – freezer friendly

INGREDIENTS

Chili is the perfect meal any time of the year, so why not on Pesach? The coffee enriches the flavor of the chili, and the two types of meat give it so much texture.

2 Tablespoons olive oil

1 large onion, diced

1 pound ground beef

1 pound boneless beef, cut into bite-size chunks

1 jalapeño pepper, seeded and finely chopped

4 Tablespoons cumin

3 Tablespoons paprika

1 Tablespoon chili powder

1 Tablespoon garlic powder

pinch cayenne pepper

½ teaspoon red pepper flakes

2 Tablespoons tomato paste

2 teaspoons kosher salt

1 Tablespoon brown sugar

1 (28-ounce) can diced tomatoes, with their liquid

2 Tablespoons instant coffee granules

2 cups warm water

METHOD

1 Heat oil in a large pot over medium-high heat. Add onion; cook for approximately five minutes, until soft and translucent.

2 Add meats and jalapeño (discard jalapeño ribs if you like your chili less hot); cook for 2-3 minutes, stirring frequently to break up the ground beef.

3 Add cumin, paprika, chili powder, garlic powder, cayenne pepper, red pepper flakes, tomato paste, salt, and sugar. Stir to coat all the meat.

4 Add diced tomatoes with their liquid. Dissolve coffee granules in water; add to the pot. Bring the mixture to a boil, then reduce heat to low; simmer for 60-90 minutes, covered, until the meat is tender.

Cook's Tip Serve chili with sliced or diced avocado and salsa. You can serve with chips for crunch, as well.

Year 'Round When making this recipe during the year, see page 235 for non-Passover alternatives.

Pastrami Meatballs

meat – yields 8-10 servings – freezer friendly

INGREDIENTS

2 pounds ground beef

6 ounces pastrami, very finely chopped

2 eggs

3 Tablespoons ketchup

1 teaspoon garlic powder

1 teaspoon onion powder

½ teaspoon dried oregano

Sauce

2 (32-ounce) jars marinara sauce

1 cup water

1 cup sugar

juice of **2** lemons (about ½ cup)

1 Tablespoon tomato paste

1 (14-ounces) can whole berry cranberry sauce

These might look like ordinary meatballs, but they have a secret weapon inside: The finely diced pastrami mixed into the meat mixture doesn't just add incredible flavor to the meatballs, but it keeps them extremely moist and soft. They're like no meatballs you've ever had before!

METHOD

1 **Prepare the meatballs:** Mix together all meatball ingredients in a large bowl until combined. Set aside.

2 **Prepare the sauce:** In a large saucepan, stir together marinara sauce, water, sugar, lemon juice, tomato paste, and cranberry sauce. Bring to a boil over medium heat.

3 Roll the meat mixture into balls approximately the size of golf balls. Carefully drop balls into boiling sauce. Reduce heat to low; simmer for approximately 1 hour 30 minutes.

Cook's Tip

• If there's any leftover sauce, freeze it and use it to make meatballs a second time!

• You can also use this meat mixture to form patties and grill them as burgers.

Bobby's Stuffed Cabbage

meat – yields 2 dozen – freezer friendly

INGREDIENTS

3 heads cabbage

Meat Filling

5 pounds ground beef

4 cloves garlic, crushed

3 eggs

1 Tablespoon paprika

1 Tablespoon kosher salt

¼ teaspoon pepper

¼ cup ketchup

Sauce

2 (46-ounce) cans tomato juice

1 cup ketchup

2 Tablespoons tomato paste

juice of **3** lemons

2 cups brown sugar

4 marrow bones

Cook's Tip

The marrow bones really make the sauce stand out with a deep and meaty flavor. If you don't have any, you can make the sauce without them.

Many people think you can't have stuffed cabbage on Pesach because they think it needs rice. That's never been a problem for me, though, because I don't like rice at all! I make delicious stuffed cabbage without rice all year long — so this version is ... perfect for Pesach.

METHOD

1 **Prepare the cabbage leaves:** Steam cabbage in boiling water for approximately 20 minutes, until the outer leaves soften and separate.

2 Drain cabbage; set aside to cool.

3 Separate the leaves; remove and discard the thick core. Trim thick ribs from leaves.

4 **Prepare the meat filling:** Combine meat, garlic, eggs, paprika, salt, pepper, and ketchup in a large bowl, mixing well. Set aside.

5 **Prepare the sauce:** Combine all sauce ingredients in large pot over medium heat. Bring to a boil; reduce to a simmer.

6 **Assemble the stuffed cabbage:** Place a handful (approximately ¼ cup, depending on the size of the leaf) of meat filling in the center of a leaf; roll up and tuck in sides. Repeat with remaining cabbage leaves and meat.

7 Place stuffed cabbage into prepared sauce. If you have leftover filling, roll it into meatballs and cook them in the sauce as well. If you have leftover cabbage, shred it and add it to the prepared sauce.

8 Cook on low for 2 hours, or until cabbage is tender.

Meltaway Spare Ribs

meat – yields 8 servings – freezer friendly

INGREDIENTS

2 large onions, sliced

5 pounds short ribs

½ cup brown sugar

1 Tablespoon fish-free imitation Worcestershire sauce

1 Tablespoon imitation soy sauce

4 cloves garlic, crushed

3 cups ketchup

½ cup water

When I first came to America as a single, I lived with the family of Mr. Moshe and Mrs. Sarah Newman, a"h, of Flatbush. After I was married, they often invited me and my family for Shabbat. These delicious spare ribs were a specialty of Mrs. Newman, and making them reminds me of her hospitality and kindness.

METHOD

1 Place onions into a large roasting pan; lay meat over onions. Set aside.

2 In a medium mixing bowl, combine sugar, Worcestershire sauce, soy sauce, garlic, ketchup, and water. Pour sauce over meat.

3 Preheat oven to 325°F. Cover ribs; bake for 3 hours, until very tender. Baste with pan juices before serving

Dairy

Quinoa Granola Parfait

dairy – yields 12 servings

INGREDIENTS

Granola Clusters

¾ cup walnuts, chopped

¾ cup pecans, chopped

¾ cup slivered almonds

¾ cup dried apples, diced

½ cup dried apricots, diced

1 cup quinoa, uncooked

¼ cup honey

¼ cup brown sugar

½ teaspoon kosher salt

1 teaspoon cinnamon

½ teaspoon imitation vanilla extract

2 Tablespoons oil

6 (6-ounce) containers yogurt, flavor of your choice

This makes the perfect breakfast. It's great plain or on the go. These aren't just for breakfast though; keep these granola clusters around as a healthier pareve snack alternative.

METHOD

1 **Prepare the granola clusters:** Preheat oven to 300°F. Line a baking sheet with parchment paper.

2 Combine nuts, fruit, and quinoa on prepared baking sheet; set aside.

3 In a small bowl, whisk together honey, brown sugar, salt, cinnamon, vanilla, and oil until smooth. Pour over the fruit/nut mixture; toss until everything is coated and sticky.

4 Bake for 30 minutes, stirring halfway through. The granola will be soft when it comes out of the oven, but will harden as it cools.

5 Set aside to cool completely.

6 Layer yogurt and granola clusters in small cups or bowls.

7 Store extra granola in a ziplock bag.

Prepare Ahead

This granola can be kept in a ziplock bag for approximately 1 week.

Year 'Round

When making this recipe during the year, see page 235 for non-Passover alternatives.

Cook's Tip

• For best results, cut all nuts and fruit into uniformly sized pieces. This will ensure that they bake evenly and have a great texture.

• You can play around with the nuts and fruits in this recipe. Try adding chocolate chips, dried cranberries, and/or your favorite nuts instead of those listed.

Almond Butter
Banana Pancakes

dairy – yields about 12 pancakes

INGREDIENTS

2 ripe bananas

4 eggs

½ cup almond butter

1 teaspoon imitation vanilla extract

1 cup chocolate chips

• butter, for frying

• honey, optional, for serving

My daughter Simi is very health conscious, and she makes these pancakes (sans the chocolate!) as a healthy breakfast. I like to add the chocolate chunks for extra flavor and texture.

METHOD

1 Place banana, eggs, almond butter, and vanilla into the bowl of a food processor fitted with the "S" blade or into a blender; blend until smooth and thick. Add chocolate chips, stirring them in with a spoon.

2 Heat a small (7-inch) nonstick frying pan over low heat. Melt butter to thinly coat bottom of pan.

3 Pour approximately ¼-cup of batter into hot pan; fry for 2-3 minutes, until the top starts to bubble (little holes will form). Flip and fry for up to 1 minute, until cooked through. Remove from pan. Repeat with remaining batter.

4 Top with honey, if using. Serve hot.

Cook's Tip

• The batter will settle after a few minutes, so stir it between every few pancakes before adding to the pan.

• To keep this recipe pareve, use cooking oil or nonstick cooking spray instead of butter.

Year 'Round

When making this recipe during the year, see page 235 for non-Passover alternatives.

Artisan Matzah Toasts

dairy – yields 4 servings – gebrochts

INGREDIENTS

1 whole matzah
• choice of toppings, below

Open-faced toasted sandwiches (or "toasts") have become super-popular, so I had to include a Pesach version using matzah. For a dairy meal, you can set up a garnish bar with small bowls of assorted garnishes. I have included my favorite topping combinations below, but you can get creative with your own combinations, using toppings such as a poached, boiled, or fried egg, tomatoes, goat or feta cheese, red onion, Greek yogurt or leben, strawberries with balsamic vinegar, beets with scallion, lox, cucumber, or just plain avocado.

METHOD

1 Divide matzah into four pieces.

2 Spread with layers of toppings of your choice. Serve immediately.

Goat Cheese & Beet Topping

INGREDIENTS

Goat cheese
sliced beets or peaches
pesto

METHOD

> Spread goat cheese on matzah. Top with very thinly sliced raw beets and a drizzle of pesto.

Avocado Feta Topping

INGREDIENTS

avocado
lemon juice
salt
sliced tomato
sliced red onion
feta cheese

METHOD

> Mash avocado together with lemon juice and salt; spread over matzah. Top with tomato, red onion, and crumbled feta cheese.

Cream Cheese & Lox Topping

INGREDIENTS

cream cheese
smoked salmon
fresh dill

METHOD

> Spread cream cheese on matzah. Top with smoked salmon and fresh dill.

Ricotta Apple Topping

INGREDIENTS

ricotta cheese
sliced apples
honey

METHOD

> Spread ricotta cheese on matzah. Top with apples and a drizzle of honey.

Shakshuka

dairy – yields 6 servings

INGREDIENTS

1 Tablespoon olive oil

1 large onion, diced

4 cloves garlic, crushed

1 (32-ounce) jar marinara sauce

1 (14-ounce) can diced tomatoes, with their liquid

1 teaspoon kosher salt

¼ teaspoon pepper

1 teaspoon cumin

6-8 eggs

• salt, to taste

• pepper, to taste

1-2 ounces feta cheese or goat cheese, crumbled

1 bunch parsley or cilantro, finely chopped, optional

This is a perfect example of my "perfect for Pesach" recipes — a year round dish that happens not to have anything that's forbidden on Pesach. This makes for a memorable breakfast or even a light lunch.

METHOD

1 Heat oil in a deep frying pan over medium heat. Add onion; sauté for 5 minutes, until soft and translucent.

2 Add garlic; continue to cook, stirring occasionally, until it is soft (2-3 minutes).

3 Add marinara sauce, diced tomatoes with their liquid, salt, pepper, and cumin. Simmer, stirring occasionally, for 5 minutes, until sauce reduces slightly and flavors are concentrated.

4 Crack an egg into a small bowl. Carefully drop the egg into the sauce. Repeat with remaining eggs, spacing them evenly around the pan. Sprinkle with salt and pepper. Cover; reduce heat. Simmer until eggs are cooked through, approximately 5 minutes for runny yolks.

5 Sprinkle cheese and parsley, if using, over shakshuka; serve immediately.

Cook's Tip

• To keep the shakshuka pareve, omit cheese.

• For a heartier meal, add 1 cup cooked quinoa and 3 cups baby spinach, which wilts into the sauce.

Prepare Ahead

Make the sauce ahead of time and store in the fridge or freezer. Heat it up in a pan; then continue with step 4.

Year 'Round

When making this recipe during the year, see page 235 for non-Passover alternatives.

Zucchini Onion Frittata

dairy – yields 4-6 servings – freezer friendly

INGREDIENTS

2 Tablespoons butter

2 Tablespoons oil

1 medium onion, cut into half-moons

2 medium zucchini, thinly sliced

½ cup grated Parmesan cheese, divided

8 large eggs

¼ cup milk

1 teaspoon kosher salt

½ teaspoon ground black pepper

¼ cup chopped fresh basil

A healthy breakfast or light lunch, frittata is basically a crustless quiche.

METHOD

1 Melt butter with oil in a large ovenproof skillet over medium-high heat; add onion and sauté until translucent, approximately 5 minutes. Add zucchini; cook for 10 minutes, until soft. Remove from heat; stir in half the grated Parmesan cheese.

2 Preheat oven to 350°F.

3 Whisk together eggs, milk, salt, and pepper until well blended. Pour over vegetable mixture in skillet.

4 Bake for 40 minutes, or until set; set oven to broil. Broil approximately 5½ inches from heat for 1-2 minutes, or until edges are lightly browned. Sprinkle evenly with remaining grated Parmesan cheese and basil.

Zoodles
with Creamy Pesto Sauce

dairy – yields 4 servings

INGREDIENTS

5 Tablespoons butter

1 clove garlic, crushed

1 teaspoon potato starch

¼ cup sour cream

2 ounces goat cheese or
    2 Tablespoons cream cheese

¼ cup prepared or homemade pesto
    (recipe below)

1½ cups milk

¼ teaspoon salt

3-4 zucchini, prepared according to
    directions on page 12

• poached egg, optional
    (see Cook's Tip)

• grated Parmesan cheese,
    for garnish

Prepare Ahead

Sauce can be made in
advance. Rewarm; then add
zoodles and cook through.

Year 'Round

When making this recipe
during the year, see page
235 for non-Passover
alternatives.

When partnering with Natural and Kosher Cheese, I developed this recipe using their goat cheese. It gives an amazing richness and creaminess to the sauce. Using zucchini noodles — "zoodles" — instead of pasta makes this dish not just kosher for Pesach, but low carb as well.

METHOD

1 Melt butter over low heat in a deep sauté pan. Add garlic; stir. Add potato starch; stir until the mixture thickens.

2 While stirring continuously, add sour cream, goat cheese, and pesto. Stir until thickened.

3 Slowly add in milk and salt, whisking until mixture becomes thickened (this happens when it reaches the boiling point).

4 Add zucchini noodles; stir until they are softened and evenly coated in sauce.

5 Top each serving with a poached egg, if using. Garnish with Parmesan cheese.

Homemade Basil Pesto

INGREDIENTS

3 cups packed fresh basil
    leaves

4 cloves garlic

1 cup pine nuts

1 cup olive oil

1 teaspoon salt (or more, to
    taste)

¼ teaspoon black pepper (or
    more, to taste)

METHOD

1 Combine all ingredients in a blender or food processor; blend until smooth.

2 Store leftover pesto in the fridge in an airtight container.

Cook's Tip

To poach eggs: Heat water in a deep 2-quart saucepan. Add a teaspoon of kosher salt and 2 teaspoons white vinegar. Bring to a boil over medium heat. Meanwhile, crack an egg into a small cup or ramekin. Use the handle of a large spoon to swirl the water to form a "whirlpool." Carefully drop the egg into the center of the whirlpool. Repeat with remaining egg (you can make two at a time). Turn off the heat; cover the pan for five minutes. Use a slotted spoon to remove the egg. Serve immediately.

Eggplant Parmesan

dairy – yields 6 servings – freezer friendly – gebrochts or non-gebrochts —

INGREDIENTS

2 **medium** eggplants

1 **teaspoon** kosher salt

1½ **cups** potato starch

3 eggs

1 **teaspoon** water

2 **cups** matzah meal

1 **teaspoon** dried oregano

1 **teaspoon** garlic powder

6 **Tablespoons** oil, divided

1 **(28-ounce) jar** marinara sauce

8 **ounces** shredded mozzarella cheese

¼ **cup** grated Parmesan cheese

Cook's Tip

Eggplant can be baked rather than fried. Coat both sides with nonstick cooking spray. Bake at 400°F for 40 minutes, turning once.

Year 'Round

When making this recipe during the year, see page 235 for non-Passover alternatives.

This is a client-favorite recipe. And although generally I try not to fry food, in this case frying is really the key to make this crisp and delicious.

METHOD

1 **Prepare the eggplant:** Slice the eggplants into slices slightly thicker than ¼-inch. Place slices in a single layer on a baking sheet. Sprinkle with salt and let sit for 30-40 minutes, allowing the salt to draw bitter liquid out of the eggplant. Press a paper towel onto each slice to absorb all the liquid.

2 **Set up a breading station:** Place potato starch into a shallow bowl; set aside. Beat eggs and water together in a second bowl. Combine matzah meal, oregano, and garlic powder in a third bowl.

3 Working with one slice at a time, dredge each in potato starch, then in egg mixture to fully coat; then in matzah meal, turning to fully coat each slice.

4 Heat half the oil in a large frying pan over medium high heat. Fry eggplant in batches until golden brown on each side (flip each slice only once). Do not crowd pan. Remove from pan; set aside.

5 Wipe out the pan with a paper towel. Add remaining oil to the pan; fry remaining eggplant slices.

6 **Assemble the eggplant Parmesan:** Preheat oven to 425°F. Prepare a baking dish large enough to hold the eggplant in two layers.

7 Spread half the sauce in the prepared baking dish. Arrange half the eggplant slices over the sauce; a little overlapping is fine. Sprinkle with half the

cheeses; cover with a thin layer of sauce. Add a second layer of eggplant; sprinkle with most of the remaining cheeses and top with remaining sauce. Sprinkle a thin layer of cheese on top.

8 Bake for 15 minutes, or until the cheese is melted and golden and the sauce is bubbly.

Zucchini Ravioli
with Spinach Ricotta Filling

dairy – yields 14-16 ravioli

INGREDIENTS

4 medium zucchini

1½ cups jarred or homemade marinara sauce

Filling

1 cup part-skim ricotta cheese

¼ cup grated Parmesan cheese

1 egg

¼ cup chopped fresh spinach

2 Tablespoons chopped fresh basil

¼ teaspoon nutmeg

¼ teaspoon salt

⅛ teaspoon pepper

½ teaspoon shredded mozzarella cheese

2 Tablespoons grated Parmesan cheese

2 teaspoons olive oil

• salt, to taste

• ground black pepper, to taste

This recipe went viral on Kitchen-Tested.com, my friend Melinda Strauss' blog. She used zucchini strips in place of pasta for the ravioli wrappers to keep this dish low carb.

METHOD

1 Preheat the oven to 375°F. Prepare 2 (9 x 13-inch) baking pans.

2 Using a potato peeler, slice the two sides of each zucchini into thin flat strips, peeling until you reach the center. You will end up with 50-60 slices. Discard the outside layers that are mainly peel rather than inside flesh.

3 Spread a layer of marinara sauce into prepared pans.

4 **Prepare the filling:** In a small mixing bowl, combine the ricotta, Parmesan, egg, spinach, basil, nutmeg, salt, and pepper. Set aside.

5 **Form the ravioli:** Place two strips of zucchini side by side, slightly overlapping. Then cross two more strips perpendicularly over the first strips, creating a plus sign shape. Spoon 1 tablespoon filling into the center of the plus sign; bring the ends of the strips together, overlapping to create the ravioli (see photo). Place upside down into the baking dish to seal. Repeat with remaining zucchini and filling.

6 Sprinkle ravioli with mozzarella and Parmesan cheeses, olive oil, salt, and pepper.

7 Bake for 30 minutes, until the zucchini is al dente and the cheese on top is turning golden brown. Serve with additional marinara sauce, Parmesan, and fresh basil, if desired.

Oozy Fried Mozzarella

dairy – yields 12 servings – freezer friendly – gebrochts or non-gebrochts —

INGREDIENTS

½ cup potato starch

3 eggs, beaten

1 cup matzah meal or non-gebrochts Pesach crumbs

½ cup grated Parmesan cheese

1 Tablespoon dried parsley

1 log (16-ounce) mozzarella cheese, cut into 12 slices

• oil, for frying

• marinara sauce, optional, for serving

Ooey-gooey-cheesy deliciousness! Don't be tempted to skip the step of freezing these, or they will melt into the oil while frying and make a big mess.

METHOD

1 Line a baking sheet with parchment paper. Set aside.

2 **Set up a breading station:** Place potato starch into a shallow bowl; set aside. Place eggs into a second shallow bowl; set aside. In a third bowl, combine matzah meal, Parmesan cheese, and parsley; set aside.

3 Dredge a slice of cheese into the potato starch, then the egg, then finally the matzah meal mixture. Press gently so the crumbs adhere. Place on prepared baking sheet; repeat with remaining cheese slices. Reserve remaining eggs and crumbs.

4 Place coated cheese into the freezer for approximately 2 hours. (Do not be tempted to skip this step, as it helps prevent the cheese from oozing out while you fry it.)

5 Remove cheese from freezer and repeat the dipping process with egg and crumbs. This will result in a very crunchy coating.

6 Heat oil in a large skillet over medium high heat. Working in batches, fry cheese until golden on both sides, 1-2 minutes per side. Transfer to a paper towel-lined plate.

7 Serve with marinara sauce, if using.

Prepare Ahead

These can be frozen after Step 5. Fry them fresh straight from the freezer.

Cheesy Hash Browns

dairy – yields 8 servings

INGREDIENTS

6 large Yukon Gold potatoes, peeled

1 teaspoon salt

½ teaspoon dried oregano

1 teaspoon dried minced onion

pinch cayenne pepper

½ stick (4 Tablespoons) butter

1 cup shredded mozzarella or cheese of your choice

Buttery, cheesy, crispy potatoes. There's no better way to start a Pesach morning. (Or any other morning!)

METHOD

1 Using a box grater or food processor, shred the potatoes on the widest blade. Squeeze out liquid; place potatoes into a large mixing bowl.

2 Add salt, oregano, onion, and cayenne pepper. Mix to combine. Set aside.

3 Melt butter over medium heat in a large frying pan until hot but not browning. Be careful not to let the butter burn.

4 Add potatoes to the pan; cook, uncovered, over medium-high heat, without stirring, until the potatoes are browned on the bottom, 5-8 minutes.

5 Sprinkle shredded cheese over potatoes; cook, uncovered, for 3-5 minutes, until the cheese starts to melt.

6 Flip hash browns (potatoes may break apart). Cook for an additional 5-10 minutes, until the bottom is crispy.

7 Flip onto a serving dish; cut into wedges to serve.

Cook's Tip

• To keep this pareve, omit the cheese and substitute oil for the butter.

• For a meat meal, add shredded pastrami to the potatoes.

Ricotta Pancakes

dairy – yields 1 dozen – freezer friendly

INGREDIENTS

1½ cups ricotta cheese

½ cup milk

½ teaspoon imitation vanilla extract

2 eggs, separated

¼ cup sugar

1 cup almond flour

¼ cup potato starch

1 teaspoon baking powder

pinch kosher salt

• oil, for frying

Whenever we visit Australia, my mum makes ricotta pancakes (latkes) for our long flight back to America. I wanted to include the recipe in my book, so I created this "Perfect for Pesach" version.

METHOD

1 Place ricotta, milk, vanilla, and egg yolks into a large bowl; mix well to combine.

2 Stir in sugar, almond flour, potato starch, baking powder, and salt; mix gently until smooth.

3 In a second bowl, beat the egg whites until stiff. Fold them into the cheese mixture.

4 Heat oil in a 9-inch frying pan over low-medium heat. Drop ¼-cup scoops of batter into pan; fry for approximately 2 minutes per side, until golden brown.

Cook's Tip

Make sure the oil doesn't get too hot, because overheated oil will cause the pancakes to break apart and burn.

Year 'Round

When making this recipe during the year, see page 235 for non-Passover alternatives.

Sides

Mock Sesame Noodles

— meat or pareve – yields 8 servings —

INGREDIENTS

Asian Almond Sauce

2 Tablespoons almond butter

4 teaspoons imitation soy sauce

1 Tablespoon honey

1 Tablespoon brown sugar

juice of **1** lime (about 2 Tablespoons)

2 cloves garlic, crushed

2 teaspoons red wine

1 Tablespoon chicken broth or water

¼ cup oil

1 teaspoon salt

1 large spaghetti squash, prepared according to directions on page 13

Optional Toppings

• carrots, cut into long, thin strips

• scallions, sliced on the diagonal

• slivered almonds

It's hard to believe that sesame noodles could be made for Pesach, isn't it? This recipe uses spaghetti squash and almond butter to replace the kitniyot in sesame noodles. The result is so good, you'll find yourself making it all year.

METHOD

1 In a small pot, combine all sauce ingredients. Cook over medium heat, whisking frequently, until smooth and combined, approximately five minutes.

2 Add spaghetti squash strands; stir until all squash is coated.

3 Garnish with your choice of toppings; serve hot.

Prepare Ahead
The sauce and the squash can each be prepared ahead of time and stored separately. Rewarm together just before serving.

Year 'Round
When making this recipe during the year, see page 235 for non-Passover alternatives.

Leora's Mashed Potatoes

pareve – yields 6 servings

INGREDIENTS

2 Tablespoons olive oil

1 onion, diced

2 cloves garlic, crushed

6 Yukon Gold potatoes, peeled and boiled with **1 teaspoon** salt, until tender, drained

1 teaspoon salt

¼ cup mayonnaise

Originally, this book wasn't going to have a mashed potato recipe. I made some quick homemade mashed potatoes with caramelized onions as a garnish for a dish at the photo shoot. After the picture was taken, my youngest daughter, Leora, tasted the mashed potatoes and commented, "These are delicious!!" After that, we knew we had to include the recipe.

METHOD

1 Heat oil in a large frying pan over medium heat.

2 Add onion; sauté for approximately 10 minutes, stirring occasionally, until softened.

3 Add garlic; sauté for an additional few minutes, until onions are starting to brown. Set aside to cool.

4 Run potatoes through a ricer or press through a sieve to mash into a creamy consistency.

5 Add salt, mayonnaise, and sautéed onions. Stir to combine. Serve immediately.

Cook's Tip

Prepare extra onions and store them in a container in the fridge or freezer. Use them to save time in any recipes that call for sautéed onions.

Broccoli Kishka Kugel

pareve – yields 12 servings – freezer friendly – gebrochts or non-gebrochts –

INGREDIENTS

Kishka Layer

1 carrot, peeled

1 potato, peeled

1 stalk celery

1 small onion, peeled

⅓ cup oil

5 Tablespoons potato starch

½ cup matzah ball mix or non-gebrochts matzah ball mix

1 teaspoon kosher salt

1½ teaspoons paprika

Broccoli Layer

1 onion, finely chopped

1 (24-ounce) bag frozen broccoli, defrosted and chopped

4 eggs

¼ cup potato starch

1 cup mayonnaise

1 teaspoon onion powder

1 teaspoon kosher salt

After making a batch of kishka for my Ultimate Pesach Cholent (page 146), I tweaked the recipe and baked it under a broccoli kugel. It adds flavor and color to the dish. Everyone loved it, and a new recipe was born.

METHOD

1 Preheat oven to 350°F. Grease 1 (9x13-inch) baking pan; set aside.

2 **Prepare the kishka layer:** In the bowl of a food processor fitted with the "S" blade, puree the vegetables.

3 Add remaining kishka ingredients; stir to combine.

4 Pour kishka mixture into prepared pan. Bake for 25 minutes.

5 **Meanwhile, prepare the broccoli layer:** Add all broccoli layer ingredients to a large bowl; stir to combine.

6 Pour broccoli mixture onto baked kishka layer; bake for 55 minutes, until firm and lightly browned.

Crispy Broccoli
with Creamy Dipping Sauce

pareve – yields 6 servings

INGREDIENTS

Broccoli is one of my favorite vegetables, and this roasting method is my favorite way to prepare it. The florets become crispy, making this a perfect snack.

2 pounds (fresh or frozen and defrosted) broccoli florets

¼ cup olive oil

2 cloves garlic, crushed

1 teaspoon kosher salt

¼ teaspoon freshly ground black pepper

Creamy Dipping Sauce

1 cup mayonnaise

¼ cup silan or honey

2 Tablespoons balsamic vinegar

½ teaspoon kosher salt

METHOD

1 Preheat oven to 425°F. Line two baking sheets with parchment paper; set aside.

2 Place broccoli, oil, garlic, salt, and pepper into a large bowl; toss until evenly coated. Spread in a single layer on prepared baking sheets.

3 Roast for 25-30 minutes for fresh broccoli (or 45-50 minutes for defrosted frozen broccoli), until broccoli starts to turn brown and crispy.

4 **Meanwhile, prepare the dipping sauce:** Add mayonnaise, silan, vinegar, and salt to a small bowl; whisk to combine. Serve alongside the broccoli.

Cook's Tip

If serving this with a dairy meal, sprinkle 2 tablespoons Parmesan cheese over the broccoli before baking.

Crispy Potato Stacks

pareve – yields 6-8 servings

INGREDIENTS

¼ cup olive oil

1½ teaspoons kosher salt

½ teaspoon paprika

½ teaspoon garlic powder

½ teaspoon onion powder

¼ teaspoon freshly ground black pepper

4 medium russet potatoes (about 2½ pounds), with peel, washed well

1 Tablespoon coarse sea salt, for garnish

These present really well and they have an amazing crispy texture, thanks to the stacked cooking method.

METHOD

1 Preheat oven to 425°F. Line a baking sheet with parchment paper; set aside.

2 In a large bowl, whisk together olive oil, salt, paprika, garlic powder, onion powder, and pepper.

3 Use a mandolin or a sharp knife to thinly slice the potatoes. Add potato slices to oil mixture; toss to coat evenly.

4 Stack potatoes in towers of 6-8 slices on prepared baking sheet. Bake for 30-35 minutes, until the tops are golden brown and the centers of the potato stacks are tender.

5 Sprinkle tops with coarse sea salt before serving.

Ratatouille

pareve – yields 8-10 servings – freezer friendly

This traditional French dish is a great vegetable side dish for Yom Tov; as a bonus, it can be prepared ahead of time and frozen.

INGREDIENTS

3 Tablespoons olive oil

1 onion, diced

4 cloves garlic, peeled and sliced

1 small eggplant, cut into ½-inch pieces

6 small zucchini cut into half-moons

1 red bell pepper, diced

1 teaspoon kosher salt

1 (28-ounce) jar marinara sauce

1 (28-ounce) can crushed tomatoes

1 teaspoon dried basil

¼ teaspoon ground black pepper

METHOD

1   Heat oil in a medium pot over medium-low heat. Add onion and garlic. Cook, stirring occasionally, until the onion has softened, approximately 5-8 minutes.

2   Add eggplant; cook, stirring occasionally, for an additional 8-10 minutes, until softened.

3   Add zucchini, red pepper, and salt. Cook until tender, 5-7 minutes.

4   Add marinara sauce and tomatoes with their liquid. Increase heat to high; bring mixture to a boil.

5   Reduce heat to a simmer; cook for approximately 40 minutes, until the vegetables are soft. Stir in basil and black pepper.

Cook's Tip

• This versatile recipe can be served hot or at room temperature.

• This recipe doubles really well, so make some extra to keep in your freezer.

Roasted Sweet Potato Wedges

pareve – yields 6-8 servings

INGREDIENTS

5 sweet potatoes, peeled and cut into wedges

3 Tablespoons olive oil

1 teaspoon garlic powder

1 teaspoon paprika

1 teaspoon kosher salt

1 teaspoon dried parsley

¼ teaspoon freshly ground black pepper

My daughter Eliana makes this all the time — it's her signature dish. Whenever she is invited to a seudah, the host requests that she bring this side dish.

METHOD

1 Preheat oven to 400°F. Line a baking sheet with parchment paper.

2 Place potato wedges on prepared baking sheet. Set aside.

3 Mix oil and spices in a small bowl to combine. Toss mixture with potato wedges until all are evenly coated.

4 Bake for 45 minutes, until the outsides are crispy and the insides are soft.

Cook's Tip

• Make sure potatoes are spread apart on the pan and not overcrowded, or the vegetables will steam and not get crisp around the edges. This is a great general rule for roasting vegetables.

• Change up the flavors of this recipe by substituting your favorite spices, such as onion powder, cumin, curry powder, smoked paprika, and cinnamon.

Cauliflower Fried "Rice"

meat or pareve – yields 6 servings

INGREDIENTS

2 Tablespoons olive oil

1 medium onion, chopped

1 Tablespoon fresh ginger, minced

3 cloves garlic, crushed

2 medium carrots, diced (about 1 cup)

4 scallions, thinly sliced

2 Tablespoons imitation soy sauce

½ pound cooked meat, chicken, corned beef, or pastrami, shredded

2 large eggs, beaten and scrambled in a small sauté pan

1 batch cauliflower "rice," prepared according to directions on page 28

¼ cup chopped almonds, or other nut (optional)

• salt, to taste

• pepper to taste

With imitation Pesach soy sauce improving over the years, it's really nice to have Asian dishes on the menu for Pesach. Feel free to switch up the vegetables and use your favorites in place of those used here. This recipe is a great way to use up leftover chicken or meat. You can also omit the chicken or meat for a pareve side dish.

METHOD

1 Heat olive oil in a sauté pan over medium heat. Add onion; sauté until soft, approximately 5 minutes. Reduce heat to low.

2 Add ginger, garlic, carrots, and scallions. Sauté on low until vegetables are soft, 5-7 minutes.

3 Add soy sauce, meat, and eggs. Stir in cauliflower "rice" and nuts, if using. Season with salt and pepper to taste.

Cook's Tip

If you can't find frozen cauliflower, prepare this with fresh: Put two heads of cauliflower through the food processor, then place into a bowl and cover with water. Microwave or boil in a pot until soft, then drain and squeeze dry according to the instructions for frozen cauliflower.

Roasted Root Vegetables
with Spiced Pecan Crunch

pareve – yields 6 servings

INGREDIENTS

3 medium potatoes, peeled and cut into large bite-size pieces

4 medium carrots, peeled and cut into large bite-size pieces

3 small parsnips, peeled and cut into large bite-size pieces

½ butternut squash, peeled and cut into large bite-size pieces

1 head garlic, broken into individual cloves, peeled

½ cup olive oil

1 teaspoon kosher salt

¼ teaspoon freshly ground black pepper

Spiced Pecans

1 cup pecans, chopped into small pieces

1 teaspoon cinnamon

¼ cup sugar

1 teaspoon ground nutmeg

The sweet spiced nuts in this dish really add a lovely crunch to the roasted vegetables, making this dish unique and delicious.

METHOD

1   Preheat oven to 400°F. Line a baking sheet with parchment paper.

2   Place all vegetables on prepared baking sheet. Toss with olive oil, salt, and pepper.

3   **Prepare the spiced pecans:** In a small bowl, combine pecans and spices. Sprinkle over vegetables.

4   Cover with foil; bake for 45 minutes until fork tender, stirring every 15 minutes.

Cook's Tip You can substitute sweet potatoes for butternut squash.

Yaptzik
(Overnight Potato and Meat Kugel)

meat – yields 10 servings – freezer friendly

This is a traditional Pesach dish of unknown origin. The slow-baked overnight potato kugel is improved only by the delicious meat hiding on the bottom.

INGREDIENTS

3 strips flanken

8-10 large potatoes

1 large onion

4 eggs, lightly beaten

1 Tablespoon kosher salt

¼ teaspoon white pepper

½ cup water

METHOD

1 Preheat oven to 350°F. Prepare 1 (9 x13-inch) pan or ovenproof baking dish.

2 Place meat into prepared pan. Set aside.

3 Using a food processor fitted with the thin shredder blade or kugel blade, shred potato and onion. Add eggs. Add salt and pepper; pour mixture over the meat.

4 Bake for 1 hour 30 minutes; then reduce oven temperature to 200°F. Pour water over kugel, cover tightly with foil, and bake for 12-16 hours, or until ready to serve.

Cook's Tip

This makes an easy substitute for cholent on Pesach and all year 'round as well!

Prepare Ahead

Bake at 350°F for 90 minutes; then remove from oven and refrigerate (or even freeze!). The morning prior to the day you plan to serve it, take the yaptzik out of the freezer; leave it in the fridge until candle lighting. Then pour approximately ½ cup of hot water onto the yaptzik. Cover it tightly with heavy-duty foil (or double-wrap with regular foil) and place overnight in the oven at 200°F. Take out of the oven right before serving at lunch the next day.

Roasted Asparagus
with Lemon & Almonds

pareve – yields 4-6 servings

This is my dressed-up Yom Tov version of simple roasted asparagus.

INGREDIENTS

2 bunches green asparagus, cleaned and trimmed

2 Tablespoons olive oil

1 teaspoon kosher salt

¼ teaspoon freshly ground black pepper

¼ cup sliced almonds

½ lemon

METHOD

1 Preheat oven to 400°F. Line a baking sheet with parchment paper.

2 Place asparagus on prepared baking sheet; drizzle with oil, salt, and pepper.

3 Bake for 15-20 minutes, depending on the thickness of the asparagus, until they start to brown. Sprinkle with almonds halfway through the baking time. Remove from oven; squeeze lemon juice over the asparagus. Serve hot or at room temperature.

Cook's Tip

A bonus in this recipe is that you can skip the step of toasting the almonds, as they toast during the cooking process.

Apple Kugel Muffins

pareve – yields 2 dozen muffins or 1 (9x13-inch) pan – freezer friendly – gebrochts –

INGREDIENTS

Filling

5 Granny Smith apples, peeled, cored, and diced

2 Tablespoons lemon juice

2 Tablespoons sugar

2 teaspoons cinnamon

Batter

5 eggs

¾ cup oil

1 cup potato starch

½ cup matzah meal

¾ cup sugar

dash kosher salt

Topping

½ cup ground almonds

1 teaspoon cinnamon

¼ cup sugar

This is a totally different take on apple crumble or kugel, with the delicious batter baking on top of the apples. I love the mini muffins for a beautiful presentation, but you can save time by baking one big kugel in a 9x13-inch pan instead. I make this recipe in large quantities as muffins. They are great for a snack, afternoon tea, or a picnic.

METHOD

1 Preheat oven to 350°F. Grease or line muffin pans or 1 (9x13-inch) baking pan; set aside.

2 **Prepare the filling:** Combine all ingredients in a medium bowl. Set aside.

3 **Prepare the batter:** Combine all ingredients in a second medium bowl. Whisk until smooth. Set aside.

4 **Prepare the topping:** Combine all ingredients in a small bowl. Stir to combine. Set aside.

5 Fill muffin cups approximately ⅔ full of apple filling, then pour batter over apples until cups are full. Sprinkle with almond topping.

6 Bake muffins for 30 minutes or 9x13-inch pan for 45 minutes, until the tops are set and lightly browned.

Shallot Potatoes

pareve – yields 8 servings

INGREDIENTS

3 Tablespoons extra-virgin olive oil

3 shallots, diced

8 Yukon Gold potatoes, peeled and cut into small dice

2 cups chicken stock

1 Tablespoon kosher salt

¼ teaspoon freshly ground black pepper

¼ cup finely chopped parsley

This dish is simple but just so delicious. Yukon Golds have a really creamy texture, which is perfect for this recipe. Shallots (a cousin of the onion) have a slightly sweet flavor, and are milder than onions — and they pair really well here.

METHOD

1 Heat the oil in a heavy-bottomed 5-quart saucepan over medium heat. Add shallots; sauté, stirring, for approximately 4 minutes, until soft and translucent, but not browned.

2 Add potatoes; continue cooking several minutes longer, stirring to ensure that the potatoes are coated well with oil and shallots.

3 Add stock; bring to a boil. Add salt and pepper.

4 Reduce heat to low; cover. Cook for approximately 20 minutes. The potatoes should be tender and have absorbed most of the stock. Fold in parsley; serve warm.

Cook's Tip

I always make this on Erev Shabbat or Yom Yov when I have chicken soup cooking next to my potatoes; I use some soup instead of stock. The chicken soup packs an extra punch of flavor to the potatoes.

Zucchini Kugel

pareve – yields 8-10 servings – freezer friendly – gebrochts

INGREDIENTS

6 medium zucchini, with peel, grated

1 onion, grated

4 eggs, beaten

1½ cups matzah meal

1 Tablespoon baking powder

¾ cup oil

1 Tablespoon kosher salt

¼ teaspoon ground black pepper

This is one of the most frequently requested recipes since I started my Pesach catering business. It's a lower-carb kugel option that everyone enjoys.

METHOD

1 Preheat oven to 350°F. Prepare 1 (9x13 inch) baking pan.

2 Add all ingredients to a large bowl; stir well to combine.

3 Pour into prepared pan. Bake, uncovered, for 90 minutes, until lightly browned and center is firm.

Desserts

Pavlova

pareve – yields 10 servings

INGREDIENTS

4 egg whites

1 cup sugar

1 teaspoon vinegar

2 teaspoons potato starch, sifted

Topping

1 (16-ounce) container nondairy whipped topping

6 strawberries, sliced

2 kiwis, peeled and sliced

I couldn't write a Pesach cookbook without including this famed Australian dessert that just happens to be ... "Perfect for Pesach!"

METHOD

1 Preheat oven to 250°F. Line a baking sheet with parchment paper; set aside.

2 In bowl of an electric mixer fitted with the whisk attachment, beat egg whites until soft peaks form.

3 Add sugar, vinegar, and sifted potato starch; beat until a soft and glossy meringue forms.

4 Pour the meringue mixture onto prepared parchment paper, shaping it into a large circle with a narrow rim.

5 Bake for 90 minutes, or until crisp on the outside.

6 Turn off oven and allow the meringue to cool inside the oven for several hours.

7 **Prepare the topping:** In the bowl of an electric mixer fitted with the whisk attachment, beat topping until stiff peaks form.

8 Immediately before serving, spread whipped topping over the top of the cooled meringue shell. Top with fruit.

Prepare Ahead

Bake meringue up to a week in advance and store airtight at room temperature.

Cook's Tip

• Feel free to replace the strawberries and kiwis with the fruit of your choice.

• To make a layered Pavlova as shown in the photo, double both the meringue and whipped cream. No need to double the fruit, as that only goes on the top layer.

• You can make these as mini pavlovas. Form meringue into 2-3-inch circles and bake at 250°F for 30 minutes.

Pomegranate Pistachio Semifreddo

pareve – yields 10 servings – freezer friendly

INGREDIENTS

1 cup nondairy whipped topping

3 eggs, separated

1 cup white sugar, divided

2 teaspoons imitation vanilla extract

½ cup pomegranate seeds

½ cup unsalted shelled pistachios, roughly chopped

Optional Garnishes

• additional pomegranate seeds

• additional whole pistachios

My mother, Miriam Stein of Sydney, Australia, is the Pesach dessert queen. At the Pesach program that my parents ran, she was always in charge of desserts. This is one of her signature recipes.

Semifreddo means semi-cold; it has a texture that's somewhere between ice cream and whipped cream.

METHOD

1 Prepare 1 (9 x 13-inch) pan.

2 In an electric mixer fitted with the whisk attachment, whip topping until stiff peaks form, approximately 5 minutes.

3 Transfer the whipped cream to a bowl. Wash and thoroughly dry the mixer bowl; change to the beater attachment. Add egg yolks and ½ cup sugar to the bowl. Mix on medium speed until the eggs are lemon colored, approximately 2 minutes. Add vanilla; beat to combine.

4 Use a spatula to gently fold the egg yolk mixture into the whipped cream.

5 Again wash and thoroughly dry the mixer bowl; change to the whisk attachment. Add the egg whites; beat on medium-high speed while slowly adding the remaining ½ cup of sugar, until stiff peaks form, approximately 5 minutes.

6 Use a spatula to gently fold the whipped egg whites into the whipped cream-egg yolk mixture.

7 Fold in the pomegranate seeds and chopped pistachios; pour mixture into prepared pan. Cover with parchment paper; then cover parchment paper tightly with foil to seal. Place in freezer for 4 hours.

Cook's Tip

If you prefer, substitute chocolate chips, mint chips, assorted nuts, coconut, marshmallow, nougat, etc. for the pomegranate seeds and whole pistachios.

8   Spoon semifreddo into serving dishes. Garnish with pomegranate seeds and whole pistachios, optional.

Cinnamon Wine Sponge Cake

pareve – yields 1 large cake – freezer friendly – gebrochts

INGREDIENTS

12 eggs, separated

1½ cups sugar

½ teaspoon lemon juice

½ cup sweet red wine

1 cup matzah cake meal

½ cup potato starch

1 teaspoon cinnamon

This is the first Pesach cake I learned how to make, and it's bursting with all the flavors we associate with this Yom Tov. My children yearn all year long for Pesach because they can't wait for me to make this cake.

METHOD

1 Preheat oven to 350°F. Grease 1 (10-inch) tube pan or 1 (9x13-inch) baking pan well; set aside.

2 In the bowl of an electric mixer fitted with the whisk attachment, beat egg yolks until light. Add sugar, lemon juice, and wine; mix well. Stir in cake meal and potato starch.

3 In a second bowl, with a clean whisk, beat egg whites until stiff; fold into batter.

4 Transfer ⅓ of the batter to a small bowl; blend in cinnamon.

5 Spoon cinnamon and white batter alternately into prepared pan to make a marble effect. Swirl the cake with a knife to get a pretty marbled effect.

6 Bake for approximately 1 hour, until a toothpick inserted in the center comes out clean and top is nicely browned.

Blueberry Cobbler

pareve – yields 8 servings in 1 (9-inch) round pan or 8-10 ramekins – freezer friendly –

INGREDIENTS

Blueberry Base

3 pints (6 cups) blueberries

½ cup sugar

½ Tablespoon cinnamon

2 Tablespoons potato starch

juice of **1** lemon (about 3 Tablespoons)

Crumbs

2½ cups potato starch

1 cup sugar

1 egg

1 cup oil

2 cups ground almonds or nut of your choice

This warm dessert is perfect comfort food any time of the year, from a summer afternoon to a winter evening. Serve it with a scoop of vanilla ice cream for a little extra indulgence.

METHOD

1 Preheat oven to 350°F. Prepare 1 (9-inch) round pan or 8-10 ramekins.

2 **Prepare the blueberry base:** Combine blueberries, sugar, cinnamon, potato starch, and lemon juice in a bowl. Toss to coat evenly. Place mixture into prepared round pan or divide among prepared ramekins. Set aside.

3 **Prepare the crumbs:** Combine all crumb ingredients; mix with a fork until coarse crumbs form. Spread the mixture over fruit base in prepared pan or ramekins. To prevent spillage, don't overfill pan(s).

4 Bake for 60 minutes for 9-inch pan and 45 minutes for ramekins, until the tops are golden brown and crisp.

Cook's Tip To take advantage of seasonal fruits, substitute 6 cups of fruit(s) of your choice, such as apples, peaches, nectarines, pears, plums, etc. in place of the blueberries.

Mini Lemon Curd Trifles

pareve – yields 6-8 servings – freezer friendly

INGREDIENTS

1 cup lemon juice

1 cup sugar

2 eggs

2 egg yolks

• crushed ladyfingers or cookie crumbs, for layering, optional

My daughter Gabi loves lemon curd, so I wanted to include a recipe for it here. I love this version because it has no margarine or hydrogenated oils. Layer the curd with crushed ladyfingers or cookie crumbs for a show-stopping dessert.

METHOD

1 In a small saucepan, combine lemon juice and sugar. Cook over low heat, stirring, until sugar has dissolved, forming simple sugar syrup. Set aside to cool completely at room temperature or in the fridge.

2 In a small bowl, lightly beat eggs and egg yolks. Slowly add beaten eggs into cold sugar syrup in the saucepan.

3 Heat over low heat for 5 minutes, stirring constantly, until bubbles begin to form at the edges. Do not bring to a boil.

4 Remove from heat; press through a strainer into a bowl to remove any curdled eggs. Set aside to cool.

5 Serve lemon curd in individual dessert cups, or layer lemon curd and crushed ladyfingers in tall glasses, as shown. Serve chilled.

Cook's Tip

Make sure the syrup is cold before you add the eggs, or the heat of the syrup will cook the eggs.

Fudgy Chocolate Bundt Cake
with Coffee Glaze

pareve – yields 1 large Bundt cake – freezer friendly

I really wanted to include a chocolate cake recipe in my cookbook. My team and I made and tested batch after batch of chocolate cakes as we fine-tuned the recipe to come up with the best Pesach chocolate cake. Our efforts have resulted in this "Perfect for Pesach" chocolate cake.

INGREDIENTS

2½ cups almond flour

1 cup cocoa powder

½ cup potato starch

1 Tablespoon instant coffee granules

1½ teaspoons baking powder

½ teaspoon kosher salt

1½ cups sugar

½ cup oil

1 Tablespoon imitation vanilla extract

6 eggs

METHOD

1   Preheat oven to 350°F. Grease a Bundt pan well; set aside.

2   In a small bowl, whisk together almond flour, cocoa powder, potato starch, coffee, baking powder, and salt. Set aside.

3   In a separate bowl, whisk together sugar, oil, vanilla, and eggs. Add dry ingredients; stir to combine.

4   Pour batter into Bundt pan; bake 40-45 minutes, until toothpick inserted into the center comes out clean. Set aside to cool completely in the pan. Remove from pan; glaze with Coffee Glaze, below.

Cook's Tip

This cake can also be baked in a 9 x 13-inch baking pan. Bake at 350°F for 35-40 minutes. Cool before glazing.

Coffee Glaze

INGREDIENTS

1 cup powdered sugar

1 Tablespoon brewed coffee

1 teaspoon oil

METHOD

1   In a small bowl, whisk together all ingredients to form a glaze. If the glaze is too thick to pour, add water, ½ teaspoon at a time, until desired texture is reached.

2   Pour glaze over cooled cake.

Vanilla Cupcakes

pareve – yields 8-12 cupcakes – freezer friendly

INGREDIENTS

4 eggs

1¼ cups sugar

½ cup oil

1 (3.5-ounce) box instant vanilla pudding

1 cup potato starch

This quick and easy, five-ingredient cupcake recipe is simple but really cute. It's perfect to have on hand when the kids want to snack.

METHOD

1 Preheat oven to 350°F. Line 1 (8-12 cup) cupcake pan with paper liners; set aside.

2 In the bowl of an electric mixer, beat eggs with sugar until combined. Add remaining ingredients; beat to combine.

3 Pour batter into prepared pans, filling them about ¾ full.

4 Bake 20-25 minutes, until tops are set.

5 Cool completely before topping with Vanilla Glaze, below (optional).

Vanilla Glaze

INGREDIENTS

1 cup powdered sugar

1 teaspoon oil

2-3 teaspoons water

• sprinkles, optional, for decorating

METHOD

1 In a small bowl, stir together sugar, oil and 2 teaspoons water to form a glaze. If needed, add an additional teaspoon of water to reach your desired consistency.

2 Drizzle over cooled cupcakes; top with sprinkles, if desired.

Betty's Fruit Sorbet

pareve – yields 8 servings per variety – freezer friendly

INGREDIENTS

Strawberry Sorbet

4 cups chopped frozen strawberries

½ cup oil

½ cup sugar

Kiwi Sorbet

4 cups chopped kiwi flesh, frozen

½ cup oil

½ cup sugar

Cantaloupe Sorbet

4 cups chopped cantaloupe flesh, frozen

½ cup oil

½ cup sugar

This recipe comes with special permission of the children of Betty Levy, a"h, who was a pillar of the Sydney Jewish community. She was one of my mum's best friends and like a second mother to me. She gave me this recipe fifteen years ago and swore me to secrecy. I've never shared it before. Betty passed away shortly before I started writing this book, and her children and I decided that it would be fitting to include this special secret recipe in her memory.

You can make one or all of the sorbets listed below.

METHOD

1 Allow the frozen fruit of your choice to defrost slightly. In the bowl of a food processor fitted with the "S" blade, puree the fruit. Add oil and sugar, processing thoroughly until very smooth. Even when you think it's ready, process for an additional few minutes.

2 Place the puree into a freezer-proof container; freeze for 6 hours.

3 Remove from freezer; allow to defrost slightly. Process again until smooth and creamy. Return to freezer until ready to serve.

4 Repeat process for each fruit.

Cook's Tip

• If you make more than one variety, you can layer them in a loaf pan. I use a melon baller to scoop out the sorbets and serve a few of each in a glass dessert bowl, just like Betty did.

• You can use frozen pineapple, mango, or your favorite fruit, chopped and frozen before beginning to prepare the recipe.

Rocky Road Fudge

pareve – yields 18 pieces – freezer friendly

Chana Hersh, another great friend of my mum, makes Rocky Road Fudge, which I love. It inspired me to make an American version of her Australian fudge.

INGREDIENTS

½ cup nondairy whipped topping, not whipped

1 (10-ounce) bag good-quality chocolate chips

1½ cups mini marshmallows

1 cup nuts

METHOD

1 Line 1 (8-inch) square pan with parchment paper, cutting the paper long and wide enough to overhang the sides.

2 Combine topping and chocolate in a small pot. Cook over low heat, stirring occasionally, until the chocolate has melted and the mixture is smooth.

3 Remove from heat; stir in marshmallows and nuts. Pour into prepared pan; refrigerate for a few hours, until firm.

4 Remove from fridge and cut into small squares.

Cook's Tip

• This is a very rich candy, so don't cut the pieces too big!

• You can add assorted nuts, dried fruit, cookies pieces, or cereal.

Apricot Nut Thumbprint Cookies

pareve – yields about 3 dozen cookies – freezer friendly

This delicious and pretty cookie was another collaborative effort. My foodie friends worked together with me to create the perfect Pesach cookie.

INGREDIENTS

Cookie

2 eggs

1 cup sugar

⅔ cup oil

1 teaspoon baking powder

1 teaspoon cinnamon

pinch salt

1 cup potato starch

3 cups ground almonds

Apricot Filling

½ cup apricot jam

2 Tablespoons lemon juice

½ cup finely chopped pecans

Prepare Ahead

Cookies can be made ahead and frozen. Freeze between layers of parchment paper so they don't stick together.

METHOD

1 Preheat oven to 350°F. Line two baking sheets with parchment paper; set aside.

2 In the bowl of an electric mixer, beat eggs together on high speed for approximately 5 minutes, until thick and foamy.

3 Add sugar, oil, baking powder, cinnamon, and salt. Beat until combined and creamy.

4 Add potato starch and ground almonds; beat until combined. Set aside.

5 **Prepare the filling:** Place jam, lemon juice, and pecans into a small bowl. Stir well to combine.

6 Coat your hands with nonstick cooking spray to prevent dough from sticking. Scoop out about 1 tablespoon of dough and roll into a ball between your palms. Place ball onto prepared baking sheet. Repeat with remaining dough.

7 Use your thumb or the back of a teaspoon measuring spoon to form an indentation in the center of each ball. Fill each with apricot filling.

8 Bake for approximately 12 minutes, until the tops of the cookies are set.

Chef Bryan's Chocolate Mousse

pareve – yields 1 dozen servings – freezer friendly

INGREDIENTS

3 (3.5-ounce) bars chocolate, 55% cocoa or higher (see Cook's Tip, below)

½ cup extra virgin olive oil

1½ teaspoons imitation vanilla extract

½ teaspoon instant coffee granules dissolved in **1 Tablespoon** boiling water

8 eggs, separated

½ cup sugar

1 teaspoon kosher salt

This recipe comes from my friend, executive chef Bryan Gryka, of Milt's Barbecue for the Perplexed. For the best texture, make sure to use chocolate that's at least 55% cocoa, which helps the mousse set (see Cook's Tip, below).

METHOD

1 In a double boiler or heatproof bowl fitted over a small pot of boiling water, melt together chocolate and oil.

2 Remove from stove; add vanilla and prepared coffee.

3 In a separate bowl, whip egg yolks and sugar together until fluffy and light yellow. Gently add yolks to the chocolate mixture. Set aside.

4 In a clean, dry mixing bowl, beat egg whites with salt until soft peaks form. Gently fold ⅓ of the egg whites into the chocolate mixture until incorporated. Repeat twice, using a third of the whites each time, until the mixture is smooth.

5 Spoon mixture into individual-serving jars, dessert bowls, or glasses. Place in the fridge to set for a few hours to cool before serving.

Cook's Tip

• When we first tested this recipe, the texture of the mousse was lacking. We spoke with Chef Bryan to troubleshoot the recipe; he determined that the cause of the problem was chocolate with a low cocoa content. Once we tried it again with 55% cocoa chocolate, the texture was perfect — so don't be tempted to try this with cheaper chocolate!

• For a more elegant presentation, Top mousse with whipped cream and/ or chocolate shavings.

Chocolate Almond Butter Bark

pareve – yields 8 servings

INGREDIENTS

2 (10-ounce) bags chocolate chips, divided **½ cup** almond butter

½ cup powdered sugar

¼ cup ladyfinger crumbs

1 Tablespoon oil, if needed

This recipe comes from my friend Miriam Pascal, who's well known for her desserts. When we made this at the photo shoot, my whole production team was raving about how indulgent this candy is.

METHOD

1 Line a baking sheet with parchment paper.

2 Melt 10 ounces of chocolate chips (see Cook's Notes, below). Spread melted chips into a thin layer on prepared baking sheet. Set aside until the chocolate has hardened.

3 Meanwhile, in the bowl of a mixer, beat together almond butter, powdered sugar, and lady finger crumbs. If the mixture is too thick, add up to a tablespoon of oil until the texture is easy to spread.

4 Spread the almond butter mixture over the hardened chocolate; place the baking sheet into the fridge for approximately 30 minutes before proceeding.

5 Melt the remaining chocolate chips; pour over the almond butter layer. Spread chocolate so that all almond butter is fully covered.

6 Set aside to cool completely, until chocolate is hardened. Cut or break into bite-size pieces.

Cook's Tip

For best results when melting chocolate (for this, or any other recipe that calls for melted chocolate), do it double-boiler style. You don't need any fancy equipment. Simply boil water in a small pot, and then place the chocolate into a heatproof bowl that fits over the pot. Stir occasionally until the chocolate is melted.

Frozen Red Wine Strawberry Mousse

pareve – yields 10 (½-cup) servings – freezer friendly

INGREDIENTS

2 (16-ounce) bags frozen unsweetened strawberries

¼ cup sugar

2 Tablespoons lemon juice

½ cup sweet red wine

1 (16-ounce) container nondairy whipped topping

Cook's Tip

• You might want to double the strawberry sauce and keep some on hand to serve over brownies, sorbet, or any dessert that needs a good sauce.

• You can also make this in a 9 x 13-inch pan or freezer-proof bowl. Remove from freezer 15 minutes before serving. Just before serving, drizzle strawberry sauce over the mousse.

While strawberry mousse is a popular Pesach treat, this version packs a ton of extra flavor due to the addition of red wine. Simmering the strawberries in wine for a long time intensifies the flavor and makes this really delicious.

METHOD

1 Prepare 10 (4-ounce) mini dessert cups.

2 In a medium pot, combine strawberries, sugar, lemon juice, and wine. Bring to a boil over medium heat; then reduce heat to low.

3 Simmer for at least 30 minutes, up to 1 hour, until the liquid is reduced and the flavors are strong. (The longer the mixture simmers, the better the flavor will be.)

4 Remove from heat. Use an immersion blender or a food processor fitted with the "S" blade to puree mixture until smooth. Set aside.

5 In the bowl of an electric mixer fitted with the whisk attachment, beat topping until stiff peaks form.

6 Reserve ½ cup of the strawberry mixture for sauce.

7 **Prepare the mousse:** Gently fold remaining strawberry mixture into the whip. Mix until smooth.

8 Transfer mousse to prepared cups. Top each cup with strawberry sauce. You can serve this way or freeze it for an ice-creamy texture.

Chocolate Chip Biscotti

pareve – yields 24-30 biscotti – freezer friendly – gebrochts —

Biscotti means "twice baked," which is the technique that gives biscotti their signature crunch, making them perfect to dunk into a cup of tea after your meal.

INGREDIENTS

4 eggs

1 cup sugar

⅔ cup oil

pinch salt

2 Tablespoons potato starch

1½ cups matzah cake meal

1½ cups ground almonds or walnuts

• chocolate chips, optional

METHOD

1 Preheat oven to 350°F. Line two baking sheets with parchment paper; set aside.

2 In the bowl of an electric mixer, beat eggs well. Gradually add sugar; beat until combined.

3 Add oil, salt, potato starch, matzah cake meal, ground nuts, and chocolate chips, if using. Beat until combined. Place the dough into the fridge for approximately 15 minutes until firm.

4 Divide chilled dough into 4 equal parts; form into logs on prepared baking sheets.

5 Bake for approximately 30 minutes, until golden. While hot, carefully cut into slices. Lay slices flat on the baking pan; return to oven for another 10 minutes.

Cook's Tip

For a more elegant presentation (as seen in the photo), melt some chocolate and dip cooled biscotti into it, then set on a cooling rack to harden.

Chili Chocolate Chip Cookies

pareve – yields 2 dozen cookies – freezer friendly

INGREDIENTS

3 cups ground almonds

½ cup light brown sugar

½ cup sugar

1 Tablespoon vanilla sugar

1 teaspoon kosher salt

1 teaspoon chili powder

1 teaspoon baking powder

2 eggs, lightly beaten

1 (10-ounce) bag chocolate chips

This recipe comes from my good friend Danielle Renov, food blogger at Peas Love 'n Carrots. I added some chili to the cookies to give them a little kick.

METHOD

1 Preheat oven to 375°F. Line two baking sheets with parchment paper; set aside.

2 Mix all ingredients together in a large bowl until well combined.

3 Scoop out approximately 1 tablespoon of dough; form into a ball. Place onto prepared baking sheet. Repeat with remaining dough.

4 Bake for 12-15 minutes, until the tops are set.

Cook's Tip

For an extra burst of flavor, sprinkle a bit of coarse sea salt over the tops of the cookies before baking.

Year 'Round

Although every recipe in this book can obviously be made all year long just as written, you may wish to substitute these not-for-Pesach ingredients when it's not Pesach.

Legumes, beans, rice, and **seeds** are not used by Ashkenazic Jews on Pesach, although Sephardic Jews are permitted to eat them on the holiday.

See the individual recipes below for not-for-Pesach cooking instructions. Note that in general wherever **potato starch** is called for, flour or corn starch can be used instead, and **matzah meal** or **Pesach crumbs** can be substituted with panko crumbs or bread crumbs.

Appetizers

16 | Cauliflower Crust Lachmagine
Use store-bought pizza dough rounds.

18 | Southwestern Chicken Egg Rolls
Add 1 can each of corn and black beans (both drained) to the chicken mixture. Use egg roll wrappers in place of crepes. Serve the soup with tortilla chips.

24 | Shepherd's Pie Potato Skins
Add a cup of frozen peas to the meat mixture.

26 | Vegetable Egg Rolls
Use egg roll wrappers in place of Pesach crepes.

Dips and Salads

38 | Quinoa "Hummus"
Garnish with a sprinkle of za'atar.

40 | Matbucha
Add chopped canned fire-roasted green chili peppers.

52 | Salad Niçoise
Add thin green beans to the salad and 1 teaspoon Dijon mustard to the dressing.

58 | Israeli Salad with Shawarma Chicken Cubes
Add roasted chickpeas for crunch.

62 | Quinoa Tabouli
Instead of quinoa, use farro or bulgur wheat.

64 | Beet Salad with Candied Nuts
Add 1 teaspoon of Dijon mustard to the dressing.

Soups

74 | Roasted Tomato Soup
This soup is great with grilled cheese sandwiches.

82 | Flanken Butternut Squash Soup
Instead of potatoes, use 2 cans of chickpeas, drained.

86 | Kale, Apple, and Sausage Soup
Add a can of Great Northern beans (drained) with the broth and canned tomatoes.

Fish

90 | Fish 'n Chips
Add a teaspoon of mustard to the tartar sauce.

96 | Crispy Flounder with Pickled Onions
Use this recipe to make amazing fish tacos.

100 | Moroccan Salmon
Add a can of chickpeas with the onions while sautéing them.

Poultry

108 | Quinoa and Mushroom Stuffed Capons
Use rice in place of the quinoa.

Meat

132 | Maple Glazed Rack of Ribs
Use bourbon instead of the white wine in the sauce.

148 | Coffee Infused Chili
Replace 1 cup of the water with 1 cup of beer.

Dairy

156 | Quinoa Granola Parfait
Add sunflower seeds to the granola for extra flavor and texture.

158 | Almond Butter Banana Pancakes
Replace almond butter with peanut butter. You can also use other chip flavors, such as butterscotch, caramel, and white chocolate.

162 | Shakshuka
Sprinkle the shakshuka with za'atar; serve it with crusty bread to soak up the sauce.

166 | Zoodles with Creamy Pesto Sauce
Replace zoodles with cooked pasta.

168 | Eggplant Parmesan
If you have a pizza stone, you can bake the eggplant slices on it, instead of frying them.

176 | Ricotta Pancakes
Use 1 cup flour in place of potato starch and almond flour.

Sides

178 | Mock Sesame Noodles
Use regular spaghetti or rice noodles instead of spaghetti squash. Garnish with toasted sesame seeds.

Index

I would like to express my special gratitude to my testers.
This book would not have been possible without you. Thank you to:

Esther Anzaroot, Chanie Apfelbaum, Lauren Barbanel, Esti Berkowitz, Eitan Bernath, Sabrina Bernath, Riva Blander, Rivka Boim, Bosh, Danielle Eisenman, Aura Engel, Rena English, Cheryl Friedman, Michal Frischman, Deena Fuchs, Hindy Garfinkel, Aliza Ginsburg, Alison Gross, Naomi Gross, Atara Habib, Malkie Hirsch, Jordana Hirschel, Leah Jaroslawicz, Kayla Kay, Melissa Kaye, Feige Koegel, Eli Kohn, Elizabeth Kurtz, Angie Lenshau, Jessica Levenson, Sandy Liebowitz, Faygie Meisels, Esther Mendelevich, Shani Nissel, Ronit Orlanski, Laura Posner, Danielle Renov, Naomi Ross, Liz Rueven, Ilanit Sternberg, Elisheva Taitz, Leslie Tuchman, Shushy Turin, Naomi Wiesen, Esty Wolbe, and Danit Zerykier.